THE COMPLETE HANNUKAH HOLIDAY COOKBOOK

A Festive Cookbook for Celebrating the Festival of Lights. 100 Delicious Recipes for Traditional and Modern Hannukah Meals, Snacks, and Desserts

Eric Green

Copyright Material ©2023

All Rights Reserved

Without the proper written consent of the publisher and copyright owner, this book cannot be used or distributed in any way, shape, or form, except for brief quotations used in a review. This book should not be considered a substitute for medical, legal, or other professional advice.

TABLE OF CONTENTS

TABLE OF CONTENTS 3
INTRODUCTION 6

1. Applesauce Loaf Cake 7
2. Beef and Cabbage for Dinner 9
3. Broccoli Rice Casserole 11
4. Red Lentil Latkes 13
5. Spinach Potato Pancakes 15
6. Whole Wheat Garlic Bread Sticks 17
7. Hannukah Onion Rings 19
8. Homemade Sour Cream 21
9. Orange-Sage Olive Oil Cake 23
10. Easy Sufganiyot 25
11. Hannukah Gelt Fudge 27
12. Baked Spinach and Cheese 29
13. Butter Mint Cookies 31
14. Roasted Sweet Potatoes & Fresh Figs 33
15. Na'ama's fattoush 35
16. Baby spinach salad with dates & almonds 37
17. Roasted eggplant with fried onion 39
18. Roasted butternut squash with za'atar 42
19. Fava Bean Kuku 45
20. Raw artichoke & herb salad 48
21. Mixed Bean Salad 50
22. Lemony leek meatballs 53
23. Hannukah Kohlrabi Salad 55
24. Root vegetable slaw with labneh 57
25. Fried tomatoes with garlic 59
26. Puréed beets with yogurt & za'atar 61
27. Swiss chard fritters 63
28. Spiced Chickpeas & Vegetable Salad 65
29. Chermoula Eggplant with Bulgur & Yogurt 68
30. Fried cauliflower with tahini 71
31. Roasted Cauliflower & Hazelnut Salad 74
32. A'ja (bread fritters) 76
33. Spicy carrot salad 78
34. Hannukah Shakshuka 80
35. Butternut Squash & Tahini Spread 82
36. Spicy Beet, Leek & Walnut Salad 84
37. Charred Okra with Tomato 87
38. Burnt Eggplant with Pomegranate Seeds 89

39. Parsley & Barley Salad 91
40. Chunky zucchini & tomato salad 93
41. Tabbouleh 96
42. Roasted potatoes with caramel & prunes 98
43. Swiss Chard with Tahini, Yogurt & Buttered Pine Nuts 101
44. Hannukah Sabih 104
45. Latkes 107
46. Hannukah Falafel 109
47. Wheat Berries & Swiss Chard with Pomegranate Molasses 112
48. Hannukah Balilah 114
49. Basmati rice & orzo 116
50. Saffron Rice with Barberries, Pistachio & Mixed Herbs 118
51. Basmati & Wild Rice with Chickpeas, Currants & Herbs ... 121
52. Barley Risotto with Marinated Feta 124
53. Conchiglie with Yogurt, Peas & Chile 127
54. Mejadra 129
55. Hannukah Maqluba 132
56. Couscous with tomato and onion 136
57. Watercress & chickpea soup with rose water 138
58. Hot yogurt & barley soup 141
59. Cannellini bean & lamb soup 143
60. Seafood & Fennel Soup 146
61. Pistachio soup 149
62. Burnt Eggplant & Mograbieh Soup 152
63. Tomato & sourdough soup 155
64. Clear chicken soup with knaidlach 157
65. Spicy freekeh soup with meatballs 160
66. Lamb-Stuffed Quince with Pomegranate & Cilantro 163
67. Turnip & veal "cake" 166
68. Hannukah Stuffed onions 169
69. Hannukah Open Kibbeh 172
70. Kubbeh hamusta 175
71. Stuffed Romano Peppers 179
72. Stuffed Eggplant with Lamb & Pine Nuts 182
73. Stuffed potatoes 185
74. Stuffed artichokes with peas & dill 188
75. Roasted Chicken with Jerusalem Artichoke 191
76. Poached chicken with freekeh 193
77. Chicken with Onion & Cardamom Rice 196
78. Chopped liver 199
79. Saffron Chicken & Herb Salad 202
80. Hannukah Chicken sofrito 205

81. Hannukah Kofta B'siniyah 208
82. Beef Meatballs with Fava Beans & Lemon 211
83. Lamb Meatballs with Barberries, Yogurt & Herbs 214
84. Turkey & Zucchini Burgers with Green Onion & Cumin 217
85. Polpettone 220
86. Braised Eggs with Lamb, Tahini & Sumac 224
87. Slow-Cooked Veal with Prunes & Leek 227
88. Hannukah Lamb shawarma 230
89. Panfried Sea Bass with Harissa & Rose 233
90. Fish & caper kebabs with burnt eggplant & lemon pickle 236
91. Panfried mackerel with golden beet & orange salsa 239
92. Cod Cakes in Tomato Sauce 242
93. Grilled fish skewers with hawayej & parsley 245
94. Fricassee salad 248
95. Prawns, Scallops & Clams with Tomato & Feta 251
96. Salmon Steaks in Chraimeh Sauce 254
97. Marinated Sweet & Sour Fish 257
98. Red Pepper & Baked Egg Galettes 260
99. Hannukah Brick 263
100. Sfiha or Lahm Bi'ajeen 265

CONCLUSION 268

INTRODUCTION

Welcome to The Joy of Hannukah, the ultimate cookbook for celebrating the Festival of Lights! Hannukah is a time for family, friends, and delicious food, and this cookbook has everything you need to create memorable meals and treats that will delight your loved ones.

In this cookbook, you'll find a wide variety of traditional and modern Hannukah recipes, from classic latkes and brisket to creative twists on traditional favorites like sufganiyot (jelly doughnuts) and challah. Whether you're a seasoned cook or a novice in the kitchen, these recipes are easy to follow and will help you create delicious Hannukah meals, snacks, and desserts that everyone will love.

But The Joy of Hannukah is more than just a cookbook – it's a celebration of Jewish culture and tradition. Throughout the book, you'll learn about the history and significance of Hannukah, as well as the stories and traditions that make this holiday so special.

So whether you're looking for inspiration for your Hannukah menu or simply want to learn more about this beloved holiday, The Joy of Hannukah is the perfect companion. Let's get cooking and celebrate the Festival of Lights in style!

Hannukah, Festival of Lights, cookbook, traditional, modern, recipes, latkes, brisket, sufganiyot, challah, Jewish culture, tradition, holiday, menu, inspiration, celebration..

1. Applesauce Loaf Cake

Yield: 16 servings

INGREDIENTS
- 1/2 cup walnuts (chopped)
- 1 1/2 cup applesauce
- 1 egg
- 1 cup sugar
- 2 tablespoons oil
- 1 teaspoon vanilla extract
- 2 cups flour (all purpose)
- 2 teaspoons baking soda
- 1/2 teaspoon cinnamon (ground)
- 1/2 teaspoon nutmeg (ground)
- 1 cup raisins

INSTRUCTIONS

a) Wash hands well with soap and warm water.
b) Pre-heat the oven to 350 degrees. Grease 2 (8x4x2 inch) loaf pans.
c) Toast walnuts in an ungreased skillet pan. Stir while heating on medium-low heat for 5-7 minutes. They are done when they are brown and smell nutty. Set aside to cool.
d) Mix applesauce, egg, sugar, oil and vanilla in a large bowl.
e) Mix flour, baking soda, cinnamon, and nutmeg together in a smaller bowl.
f) Pour flour mixture into applesauce mixture.
g) Stir in raisins and cooled toasted nuts.
h) Pour half of the batter into each greased pan. Bake for 45-55 minutes.
i) Remove cakes from the oven. Cool for 10 minutes. Remove from pans to finish cooling. For best taste, let cakes cool a few hours before serving.

2. Beef and Cabbage for Dinner

Yield: 4 Servings

INGREDIENTS
- 1 green cabbage head (washed and cut into bite-sized pieces)
- 1 onion, medium (chopped)
- 1 pound ground beef, lean (15% fat)
- non-stick cooking spray
- 1 teaspoon garlic powder
- 1/4 teaspoon black pepper
- salt (to taste, optional)
- red pepper flakes (to taste, optional)

INSTRUCTIONS
a) Chop cabbage and onions, set aside.
b) In a large skillet, cook the ground beef on medium heat until browned. Drain the fat. Set beef aside.
c) Spray skillet with non-stick cooking spray. Cook onions on medium heat until soft.
d) Add cabbage to the onions and cook until cabbage starts to brown.
e) Stir the beef into the cabbage and onion mixture.
f) Season with garlic powder, salt (optional), and pepper. Add red pepper flakes (optional) to the cabbage if you like it spicy.

3. Broccoli Rice Casserole

Yield: 12 servings

INGREDIENTS
- 1 1/2 cup rice
- 3 1/2 cups water
- 1 onion (medium, chopped)
- 1 can cream of mushroom, or chicken, or celery or cheese soup (10 3/4 ounce, condensed)
- 1 1/2 cup milk (1%)
- 20 ounces broccoli or cauliflower or mixed vegetables (frozen, chopped)
- 1/2 pound cheese (grated or sliced)
- 3 tablespoons magarine (or butter)

INSTRUCTIONS
a) Preheat oven to 350 degrees and grease on 12x9x2 inch baking pan.
b) In a saucepan mix rice, salt, and 3 cups of water and bring to a boil.
c) Cover and simmer for 15 minutes. Remove saucepan from heat and set aside for additional 15 minutes.
d) Saute onions in margarine (or butter) until tender.
e) Mix soup, milk, 1/2 cup of water, onions, and rice. Spoon mixture into baking pan.
f) Thaw and drain the vegetables and then spread over the rice mixture.
g) Spread the cheese evenly over the top and bake at 350 degrees for 25-30 minutes until cheese is melted and rice is bubbly.

4. Red Lentil Latkes

Yield: 4 Servings

INGREDIENTS
- 1/2 cup dry red lentils
- 1 potato, medium grated (about 1/2 pound, peeling is optional)
- 1 large egg
- 1 garlic clove, finely sliced
- 2 tablespoons Parmesan cheese, grated or other cheese
- 1 dash hot sauce (1-2 dashes, optional)
- 1/4 teaspoon salt
- black pepper (to taste, optional)
- 2 tablespoons canola oil (or olive oil, for cooking)

INSTRUCTIONS

a) Add the lentils to a medium saucepan and add water to cover by about an inch. Bring to a boil, then lower heat to a simmer and cook until tender, about 15 minutes. Drain and set aside.

b) Meanwhile, remove the excess water from the potato: you can either squeeze it by the handful, or put the entire pile on a clean tea towel and wring it out.

c) Crack the egg in a medium bowl and beat it lightly. Add the potato, cooked lentils, garlic, green onion, and cheese and hot sauce if you're using them in a medium bowl. Add the salt and a good grinding of black pepper, and stir until combined.

d) Heat a large skillet over medium heat, then add a generous drizzle of oil (1-2 Tablespoons). Working in batches, so as not to crowd the pan, add clumps of the potato-lentil mixture (about the size of a golf ball or slightly larger works well), and flatten each as soon as it's in the pan, making them about a half inch thick.

e) Cook for about 4-5 minutes per side, until the latkes are deeply golden brown and cooked through. Add a little more oil to the pan for each additional batch. Serve immediately or keep the latkes warm in a 200°F oven for up to an hour.

5. Spinach Potato Pancakes

Yield: 4 Servings

INGREDIENTS
- 2 cups zucchini, shredded
- 1 potato, medium (peeled and shredded)
- 1/4 cup onion, finely chopped
- 1/4 teaspoon salt
- 1/4 cup whole wheat flour
- 1 1/2 cup spinach, chopped and steamed
- 1/2 teaspoon pepper
- 1/4 teaspoon ground nutmeg
- 1 egg, beaten
- applesauce (optional)

INSTRUCTIONS

a) Combine the first eight ingredients in a bowl.
b) Stir in egg and mix well.
c) Drop batter by 1/4 cup-fuls onto a well-greased hot griddle and flatten to form patties.
d) Fry until golden brown; turn and cook until the second side is lightly browned. Drain on paper towels and serve with applesauce, if desired.

6. Whole Wheat Garlic Bread Sticks

Yield: 6 servings

INGREDIENTS:
- 6 slices bread (100% whole wheat)
- 2 tablespoons olive oil
- 1/2 teaspoon garlic powder
- 1 Italian seasoning (as needed, to sprinkle on)

INSTRUCTIONS
a) Spread each slice of bread with one teaspoon oil.
b) Sprinkle with garlic powder and Italian seasoning.
c) Stack bread and cut each slice into 3 equal parts.
d) Bake at 300 degrees for about 25 minutes or until crisp and lightly browned.

7. Hannukah Onion Rings

INGREDIENTS:
- 3 large onions
- 1 cup corn meal
- 1 cup flour
- 2 teaspoons salt
- 1 cup yogurt
- 1 cup milk
- Ground pepper
- Oil for frying

INSTRUCTIONS

a) In a large pot, heat about ¾" oil to 350° F. Combine the milk and yogurt in small bowl. Combine cornmeal, flour, salt, and pepper in another bowl.
b) Slice the onions and separate the rings. Soak the rings in the milk and yogurt mixture for a few minutes.
c) Next dredge both sides through the flour mixture and use tongs to place rings into the oil. Cook the rings until they are just golden.
d) Remove to a paper towel and keep warm in 200° F oven.

8. Homemade Sour Cream

INGREDIENTS:
- ¼ cup milk
- 1 cup heavy cream
- ¾ teaspoons distilled white vinegar

INSTRUCTIONS

a) Combine the milk and vinegar and let stand for 10 minutes. Pour the heavy cream into a jar.
b) Stir in the milk mixture, cover the jar, and let stand at room temperature for 24 hours.
c) Chill before using.

9. Orange-Sage Olive Oil Cake

INGREDIENTS:
CAKE:
- 4 eggs
- 1 cup sugar
- ½ cup extra virgin olive oil
- ¼ cup orange juice
- 2 tablespoons orange zest
- 1 tablespoon finely chopped fresh sage
- 1 ½ cups all-purpose flour
- 1 tablespoon baking powder
- ½ teaspoon salt
- ½ teaspoon cinnamon

ORANGE ICING:
- 1 cup powdered sugar
- 2 tablespoons orange juice

INSTRUCTIONS

a) Preheat oven to 350° F and grease 1 large loaf pan. In a stand mixer, beat the eggs with the sugar for 2 minutes, until mixture is fluffy. With the mixer running on low, drizzle in the olive oil and orange juice. Fold in the orange zest and sage leaves.

b) In a separate mixing bowl, combine the flour, baking powder, salt, and cinnamon.

c) Add the dry mixture to the wet in the stand mixer and blend until smooth.

d) Pour the batter into the loaf pan. Bake the cake for 30-35 minutes. Set the cake aside for 15 minutes in the pan then transfer to a wire rack to cool completely.

e) In a mixing bowl, whisk together the powdered sugar and orange juice. When the cake has cooled, drizzle with the icing and set aside until the icing has set.

10. Easy Sufganiyot

INGREDIENTS:
- One roll store-bought biscuit dough
- Canola oil, for frying
- Small bowl of sugar, white or powdered
- ½ cup jam Oil

INSTRUCTIONS

a) Let dough sit at room temperature for 20 minutes, so it is easy to roll out.
b) On a floured surface, roll out dough until it is ½" thick. Cut out 2 ½" or 3" circles.
c) Fill a pot with 2" of oil and heat it to 360° F.
d) Fry the dough until each side is a deep brown. Test one to make sure they're not doughy in the middle. Transfer donuts to a paper towel, pat off any excess grease, and coat with sugar.
e) Fill with jam using a squeeze bottle.

11. Hannukah Gelt Fudge

INGREDIENTS
- 3 cups semi-sweet chocolate chips
- 1 can sweetened condensed milk
- 1 teaspoon vanilla
- ¼ teaspoon salt

INSTRUCTIONS
a) Combine chocolate chips and condensed milk in bowl and heat in microwave for 1 minute.
b) Stir until smooth. If more time is required, continue heating in microwave in increments of 10 seconds.
c) Add vanilla and salt and stir. Spread into a dish lined with waxed paper. Refrigerate for ½ hour. Cut fudge into desired shapes and wrap in foil.
d) Refrigerate fudge until ready to eat.

12. Baked Spinach and Cheese

INGREDIENTS
- Nonstick cooking spray
- 2 whole eggs plus 2 egg whites
- ¾ cup milk
- 3 slices day-old light bread, cut into small triangles
- 1 cup fresh spinach, finely chopped
- ½ cup shredded Parmesan cheese

INSTRUCTIONS

a) Preheat the oven to 350° F. Line the bottom of an 8" springform pan with baking paper and spray with nonstick cooking spray. In a medium bowl, whisk the eggs and egg whites until frothy.

b) Add the milk, spinach, and cheese. Stir to blend. Pour into the prepared pan.

c) Immerse the dried bread triangles in the mixture. After they are coated with the mixture, raise one point of each piece with a fork so that they peek out at the top.

d) Bake uncovered until lightly browned, about 20-30 minutes.

e) Remove from the oven and cool. Loosen the edges by cutting around the outside with a knife. Remove from the pan and place on a heatproof plate.

13. Butter Mint Cookies

INGREDIENTS

- 1 cup butter, softened
- ½ cup confectioners' sugar
- 1 ½ teaspoons peppermint extract
- 1 ¾ cups all-purpose flour
- Green colored sugar

INSTRUCTIONS

a) In a large bowl, cream butter and confectioners' sugar until light and fluffy. Beat in extract. Gradually add flour and mix well. Roll tablespoons of dough into balls.

b) Place 1" apart on ungreased baking sheets; flatten with a glass dipped in colored sugar. Bake at 350° F for 12-14 minutes or until firm.

c) Remove to wire racks to cool. Yield: 3 dozen.

14. Roasted Sweet Potatoes & Fresh Figs

Makes: 4

INGREDIENTS
- 4 small sweet potatoes (2¼ lb / 1 kg in total)
- 5 tbsp olive oil
- 3 tbsp / 40 ml balsamic vinegar (you can use a commercial rather than a premium aged grade)
- 1½ tbsp / 20 g superfine sugar
- 12 green onions, halved lengthwise and cut into 1½-in / 4cm segments
- 1 red chile, thinly sliced
- 6 ripe figs (8½ oz / 240 g in total), quartered
- 5 oz / 150 g soft goat's milk cheese (optional)
- Maldon sea salt and freshly ground black pepper

INSTRUCTIONS

a) Preheat the oven to 475°F / 240°C.

b) Wash the sweet potatoes, halve them lengthwise, and then cut each half again similarly into 3 long wedges. Mix with 3 tablespoons of the olive oil, 2 teaspoons salt, and some black pepper. Spread the wedges out, skin side down, on a baking sheet and cook for about 25 minutes, until soft but not mushy. Remove from the oven and leave to cool down.

c) To make the balsamic reduction, place the balsamic vinegar and sugar in a small saucepan. Bring to a boil, then decrease the heat and simmer for 2 to 4 minutes, until it thickens. Be sure to remove the pan from the heat when the vinegar is still runnier than honey; it will continue to thicken as it cools. Stir in a drop of water before serving if it does become too thick to drizzle.

d) Arrange the sweet potatoes on a serving platter. Heat the remaining oil in a medium saucepan over medium heat and add the green onions and chile. Fry for 4 to 5 minutes, stirring often to make sure not to burn the chile. Spoon the oil, onions, and chile over the sweet potatoes. Dot the figs among the wedges and then drizzle over the balsamic reduction. Serve at room temperature. Crumble the cheese over the top, if using.

15. Na'ama's fattoush

Makes: 6

INGREDIENTS

- 1 cup / 200 g Greek yogurt and ¾ cup plus 2 tbsp / 200 ml whole milk, or 1⅔ cups / 400 ml buttermilk (replacing both yogurt and milk)
- 2 large stale Turkish flatbread or naan (9 oz / 250 g in total)
- 3 large tomatoes (13 oz / 380 g in total), cut into ⅔-inch / 1.5cm dice
- 3½ oz / 100 g radishes, thinly sliced
- 3 Lebanese or mini cucumbers (9 oz / 250 g in total), peeled and chopped into ⅔-inch / 1.5cm dice
- 2 green onions, thinly sliced
- ½ oz / 15 g fresh mint
- 1 oz / 25 g flat-leaf parsley, coarsely chopped
- 1 tbsp dried mint
- 2 cloves garlic, crushed
- 3 tbsp freshly squeezed lemon juice
- ¼ cup / 60 ml olive oil, plus extra to drizzle
- 2 tbsp cider or white wine vinegar
- ¾ tsp freshly ground black pepper
- 1½ tsp salt
- 1 tbsp sumac or more to taste, to garnish

INSTRUCTIONS

a) If using yogurt and milk, start at least 3 hours and up to a day in advance by placing both in a bowl. Whisk well and leave in a cool place or in the fridge until bubbles form on the surface. What you get is a kind of homemade buttermilk, but less sour.

b) Tear the bread into bite-size pieces and place in a large mixing bowl. Add your fermented yogurt mixture or commercial buttermilk, followed by the rest of the ingredients, mix well, and leave for 10 minutes for all the flavors to combine.

c) Spoon the fattoush into serving bowls, drizzle with some olive oil, and garnish generously with sumac.

16. Baby spinach salad with dates & almonds

Makes: 4

INGREDIENTS
- 1 tbsp white wine vinegar
- ½ medium red onion, thinly sliced
- 3½ oz / 100 g pitted Medjool dates, quartered lengthwise
- 2 tbsp / 30 g unsalted butter
- 2 tbsp olive oil
- 2 small pitas, about 3½ oz / 100 g, roughly torn into 1½-inch / 4cm pieces
- ½ cup / 75 g whole unsalted almonds, coarsely chopped
- 2 tsp sumac
- ½ tsp chile flakes
- 5 oz / 150 g baby spinach leaves
- 2 tbsp freshly squeezed lemon juice
- salt

INSTRUCTIONS

a) Put the vinegar, onion, and dates in a small bowl. Add a pinch of salt and mix well with your hands. Leave to marinate for 20 minutes, then drain any residual vinegar and discard.

b) Meanwhile, heat the butter and half the olive oil in a medium frying pan over medium heat. Add the pita and almonds and cook for 4 to 6 minutes, stirring all the time, until the pita is crunchy and golden brown. Remove from the heat and mix in the sumac, chile flakes, and ¼ teaspoon salt. Set aside to cool.

c) When you are ready to serve, toss the spinach leaves with the pita mix in a large mixing bowl. Add the dates and red onion, the remaining olive oil, the lemon juice, and another pinch of salt. Taste for seasoning and serve immediately.

17. Roasted eggplant with fried onion

Makes: 4

INGREDIENTS
- 2 large eggplants, halved lengthwise with the stem on (about 1⅔ lb / 750 g in total)
- ⅔ cup / 150 ml olive oil
- 4 onions (about 1¼ lb / 550 g in total), thinly sliced
- 1½ green chiles
- 1½ tsp ground cumin
- 1 tsp sumac
- 1¾ oz / 50 g feta cheese, broken into large chunks
- 1 medium lemon
- 1 clove garlic, crushed
- salt and freshly ground black pepper

INSTRUCTIONS

a) Preheat the oven to 425°F / 220°C.
b) Score the cut side of each eggplant with a crisscross pattern. Brush the cut sides with 6½ tbsp / 100 ml of the oil and sprinkle liberally with salt and pepper. Place on a baking sheet, cut side up, and roast in the oven for about 45 minutes, until the flesh is golden brown and completely cooked.
c) While the eggplants are roasting, add the remaining oil to a large frying pan and place over high heat. Add the onions and ½ teaspoon salt and cook for 8 minutes, stirring often, so that parts of the onion get really dark and crisp. Seed and chop the chiles, keeping the whole one separate from the half. Add the ground cumin, sumac, and the whole chopped chile and cook for a further 2 minutes before adding the feta. Cook for a final minute, not stirring much, then remove from the heat.
d) Use a small serrated knife to remove the skin and pith of the lemon. Coarsely chop the flesh, discarding the seeds, and place the flesh and any juices in a bowl with the remaining ½ chile and the garlic.
e) Assemble the dish as soon as the eggplants are ready. Transfer the roasted halves to a serving dish and spoon the lemon sauce over the flesh. Warm up the onions a little and spoon over. Serve warm or set aside to come to room temperature.

18. Roasted butternut squash with za'atar

Makes: 4

INGREDIENTS

- 1 large butternut squash (2½ lb / 1.1 kg in total), cut into ¾ by 2½-inch / 2 by 6cm wedges
- 2 red onions, cut into 1¼-inch / 3cm wedges
- 3½ tbsp / 50 ml olive oil
- 3½ tbsp light tahini paste
- 1½ tbsp lemon juice
- 2 tbsp water
- 1 small clove garlic, crushed
- 3½ tbsp / 30 g pine nuts
- 1 tbsp za'atar
- 1 tbsp coarsely chopped flat-leaf parsley
- Maldon sea salt and freshly ground black pepper

INSTRUCTIONS

a) Preheat the oven to 475°F / 240°C.

b) Put the squash and onion in a large mixing bowl, add 3 tablespoons of the oil, 1 teaspoon salt, and some black pepper and toss well. Spread on a baking sheet with the skin facing down and roast in the oven for 30 to 40 minutes, until the vegetables have taken on some color and are cooked through. Keep an eye on the onions as they might cook faster than the squash and need to be removed earlier. Remove from the oven and leave to cool.

c) To make the sauce, place the tahini in a small bowl along with the lemon juice, water, garlic, and ¼ teaspoon salt. Whisk until the sauce is the consistency of honey, adding more water or tahini if necessary.

d) Pour the remaining 1½ teaspoons oil into a small frying pan and place over medium-low heat. Add the pine nuts along with ½ teaspoon salt and cook for 2 minutes, stirring often, until the nuts are golden brown. Remove from the heat and transfer the nuts and oil to a small bowl to stop the cooking.

e) To serve, spread the vegetables out on a large serving platter and drizzle over the tahini. Sprinkle the pine nuts and their oil on top, followed by the za'atar and parsley.

19. Fava Bean Kuku

Makes: 6

INGREDIENTS
- 1 lb / 500 g fava beans, fresh or frozen
- 5 tbsp / 75 ml boiling water
- 2 tbsp superfine sugar
- 5 tbsp / 45 g dried barberries
- 3 tbsp heavy cream
- ¼ tsp saffron threads
- 2 tbsp cold water
- 5 tbsp olive oil
- 2 medium onions, finely chopped
- 4 cloves garlic, crushed
- 7 large free-range eggs
- 1 tbsp all-purpose flour
- ½ tsp baking powder
- 1 cup / 30 g dill, chopped
- ½ cup / 15 g mint, chopped
- salt and freshly ground black pepper

INSTRUCTIONS

a) Preheat the oven to 350°F / 180°C. Put the fava beans in a pan with plenty of boiling water. Simmer for 1 minute, drain, refresh under cold water, and set aside.

b) Pour the 5 tbsp / 75 ml boiling water into a medium bowl, add the sugar, and stir to dissolve. Once this syrup is tepid, add the barberries and leave them for about 10 minutes, then drain.

c) Bring the cream, saffron, and cold water to a boil in a small saucepan. Immediately remove from the heat and set aside for 30 minutes to infuse.

d) Heat 3 tablespoons of the olive oil over medium heat in a 10-inch / 25cm nonstick, ovenproof frying pan for which you have a lid. Add the onions and cook for about 4 minutes, stirring occasionally, then add the garlic and cook and stir for a further 2 minutes. Stir in the fava beans and set aside.

e) Beat the eggs well in a large mixing bowl until frothy. Add the flour, baking powder, saffron cream, herbs, 1½ teaspoons salt, and ½ teaspoon pepper and whisk well. Finally, stir in the barberries and the fava beans and onion mix.
f) Wipe the frying pan clean, add the remaining olive oil, and place in the oven for 10 minutes to heat well. Pour the egg mix into the hot pan, cover with the lid, and bake for 15 minutes. Remove the lid and bake for another 20 to 25 minutes, until the eggs are just set. Remove from the oven and let rest for 5 minutes, before inverting onto a serving platter. Serve warm or at room temperature.

Raw Artichoke & Herb Salad

20. Raw artichoke & herb salad

Makes: 2

INGREDIENTS
- 2 or 3 large globe artichokes (1½ lb / 700 g in total)
- 3 tbsp freshly squeezed lemon juice
- 4 tbsp olive oil
- 2 cups / 40 g arugula
- ½ cup / 15 g torn mint leaves
- ½ cup / 15 g torn cilantro leaves
- 1 oz / 30 g pecorino toscano or romano cheese, thinly shaved
- Maldon sea salt and freshly ground black pepper

INSTRUCTIONS

a) Prepare a bowl of water mixed with half of the lemon juice. Remove the stem from 1 artichoke and pull off the tough outer leaves. Once you reach the softer, pale leaves, use a large, sharp knife to cut across the flower so that you are left with the bottom quarter. Use a small, sharp knife or a vegetable peeler to remove the outer layers of the artichoke until the base, or bottom, is exposed. Scrape out the hairy "choke" and put the base in the acidulated water. Discard the rest, then repeat with the other artichoke(s).

b) Drain the artichokes and pat dry with paper towels. Using a mandoline or large, sharp knife, cut the artichokes into paper-thin slices and transfer to a large mixing bowl. Squeeze over the remaining lemon juice, add the olive oil, and toss well to coat. You can leave the artichoke for up to a few hours if you like, at room temperature. When ready to serve, add the arugula, mint, and cilantro to the artichoke and season with a generous ¼ teaspoon salt and plenty of freshly ground black pepper.

c) Toss gently and arrange on serving plates. Garnish with the pecorino shavings.

21. Mixed Bean Salad

Makes: 4

INGREDIENTS
- 10 oz / 280 g yellow beans, trimmed (if unavailable, double the quantity of green beans)
- 10 oz / 280 g green beans, trimmed
- 2 red peppers, cut into ¼-inch / 0.5cm strips
- 3 tbsp olive oil, plus 1 tsp for the peppers
- 3 cloves garlic, thinly sliced
- 6 tbsp / 50 g capers, rinsed and patted dry
- 1 tsp cumin seeds
- 2 tsp coriander seeds
- 4 green onions, thinly sliced
- ⅓ cup / 10 g tarragon, coarsely chopped
- ⅔ cup / 20 g picked chervil leaves (or a mixture of picked dill and shredded parsley)
- grated zest of 1 lemon
- salt and freshly ground black pepper

INSTRUCTIONS

a) Preheat the oven to 450°F / 220°C.
b) Bring a large pan with plenty of water to a boil and add the yellow beans. After 1 minute, add the green beans and cook for another 4 minutes, or until the beans are cooked through but still crunchy. Refresh under ice-cold water, drain, pat dry, and place in a large mixing bowl.
c) Meanwhile, toss the peppers in 1 teaspoon of the oil, spread on a baking sheet, and place in the oven for 5 minutes, or until tender. Remove from the oven and add to the bowl with the cooked beans.
d) Heat the 3 tablespoons olive oil in a small saucepan. Add the garlic and cook for 20 seconds; add the capers (careful, they spit!) and fry for another 15 seconds. Add the cumin and coriander seeds and continue frying for another 15 seconds. The garlic should have turned golden by now. Remove from the heat and pour the contents of the pan immediately over the beans. Toss and add the green onions, herbs, lemon zest, a generous ¼ teaspoon salt, and black pepper.
e) Serve, or keep refrigerated for up to a day. Just remember to bring back to room temperature before serving.

22. Lemony leek meatballs

Makes: 4 AS A STARTER

INGREDIENTS
- 6 large trimmed leeks (about 1¾ lb / 800 g in total)
- 9 oz / 250 g ground beef
- 1 cup / 90 g bread crumbs
- 2 large free-range eggs
- 2 tbsp sunflower oil
- ¾ to 1¼ cups / 200 to 300 ml chicken stock
- ⅓ cup / 80 ml freshly squeezed lemon juice (about 2 lemons)
- ⅓ cup / 80 g Greek yogurt
- 1 tbsp finely chopped flat-leaf parsley
- salt and freshly ground black pepper

INSTRUCTIONS

a) Cut the leeks into ¾-inch / 2cm slices and steam them for approximately 20 minutes, until completely soft. Drain and leave to cool, then squeeze out any residual water with a tea towel. Process the leeks in a food processor by pulsing a few times until well chopped but not mushy. Place the leeks in a large mixing bowl, along with the meat, bread crumbs, eggs, 1¼ teaspoons salt, and 1 teaspoon black pepper. Form the mix into flat patties, roughly 2¾ by ¾ inches / 7 by 2 cm—this should make 8. Refrigerate for 30 minutes.

b) Heat the oil over medium-high heat in a large, heavy-bottomed frying pan for which you have a lid. Sear the patties on both sides until golden brown; this can be done in batches if necessary.

c) Wipe out the pan with a paper towel and then lay the meatballs on the bottom, slightly overlapping if needed. Pour over enough stock to almost, but not quite cover the patties. Add the lemon juice and ½ teaspoon salt. Bring to a boil, then cover and simmer gently for 30 minutes. Remove the lid and cook for a few more minutes, if needed, until almost all the liquid has evaporated. Remove the pan from the heat and set aside to cool down.

d) Serve the meatballs just warm or at room temperature, with a dollop of the yogurt and a sprinkle of the parsley.

23. Hannukah Kohlrabi Salad

Makes: 4

INGREDIENTS
- 3 medium kohlrabies (1⅔ lb / 750 g in total)
- ⅓ cup / 80 g Greek yogurt
- 5 tbsp / 70 g sour cream
- 3 tbsp mascarpone cheese
- 1 small clove garlic, crushed
- 1½ tsp freshly squeezed lemon juice
- 1 tbsp olive oil
- 2 tbsp finely shredded fresh mint
- 1 tsp dried mint
- about 12 sprigs / 20 g baby watercress
- ¼ tsp sumac
- salt and white pepper

INSTRUCTIONS
a) Peel the kohlrabies, cut into ⅔-inch / 1.5cm dice, and put in a large mixing bowl. Set aside and make the dressing.
b) Put the yogurt, sour cream, mascarpone, garlic, lemon juice, and olive oil in a medium bowl. Add ¼ teaspoon salt and a healthy grind of pepper and whisk until smooth. Add the dressing to the kohlrabi, followed by the fresh and dried mint and half the watercress.
c) Gently stir, then place on a serving dish. Dot the remaining watercress on top and sprinkle with the sumac.

24. Root vegetable slaw with labneh

Makes: 6

INGREDIENTS
- 3 medium beets (1 lb / 450 g in total)
- 2 medium carrots (9 oz / 250 g in total)
- ½ celery root (10 oz / 300 g in total)
- 1 medium kohlrabi (9 oz / 250 g in total)
- 4 tbsp freshly squeezed lemon juice
- 4 tbsp olive oil
- 3 tbsp sherry vinegar
- 2 tsp superfine sugar
- ¾ cup / 25 g cilantro leaves, coarsely chopped
- ¾ cup / 25 g mint leaves, shredded
- ⅔ cup / 20 g flat-leaf parsley leaves, coarsely chopped
- ½ tbsp grated lemon zest
- 1 cup / 200 g labneh (store-bought or see recipe)
- salt and freshly ground black pepper
- Peel all the vegetables and slice them thinly, about 1/16 small hot chile, finely chopped

INSTRUCTIONS

a) Place the lemon juice, olive oil, vinegar, sugar, and 1 teaspoon salt in a small saucepan. Bring to a gentle simmer and stir until the sugar and the salt have dissolved. Remove from the heat.

b) Drain the vegetable strips and transfer to a paper towel to dry well. Dry the bowl and replace the vegetables. Pour the hot dressing over the vegetables, mix well, and leave to cool. Place in the fridge for at least 45 minutes.

c) When ready to serve, add the herbs, lemon zest, and 1 teaspoon black pepper to the salad. Toss well, taste, and add more salt if needed. Pile onto serving plates and serve with some labneh on the side.

25. Fried tomatoes with garlic

Makes: 2 To 4

INGREDIENTS
- 3 large cloves garlic, crushed
- ½ small hot chile, finely chopped
- 2 tbsp chopped flat-leaf parsley
- 3 large, ripe but firm tomatoes (about 1 lb / 450 g in total)
- 2 tbsp olive oil
- Maldon sea salt and freshly ground black pepper
- rustic bread, to serve

INSTRUCTIONS

a) Mix the garlic, chile, and chopped parsley in a small bowl and set aside. Top and tail the tomatoes and slice vertically into slices about ⅔ inch / 1.5 cm thick.

b) Heat the oil in a large frying pan over medium heat. Add the tomato slices, season with salt and pepper, and cook for about 1 minute, then turn over, season again with salt and pepper, and sprinkle with the garlic mixture. Continue to cook for another minute or so, shaking the pan occasionally, then turn the slices again and cook for a few more seconds, until soft but not mushy.

c) Turn the tomatoes over onto a serving plate, pour over the juices from the pan, and serve immediately, accompanied with the bread.

26. Puréed beets with yogurt & za'atar

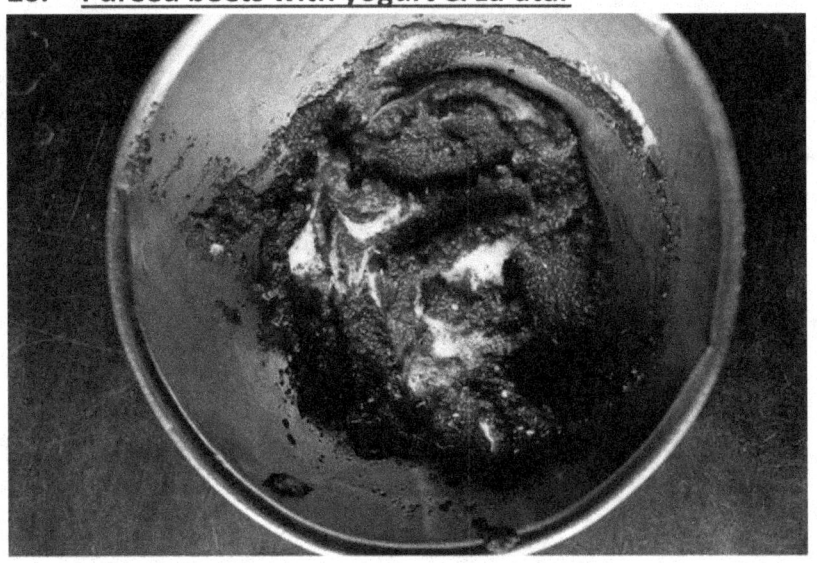

Makes: 6

INGREDIENTS

- 2 lb / 900 g medium beets (about 1 lb / 500 g in total after cooking and peeling)
- 2 cloves garlic, crushed
- 1 small red chile, seeded and finely chopped
- rounded 1 cup / 250 g Greek yogurt
- 1½ tbsp date syrup
- 3 tbsp olive oil, plus extra to finish the dish
- 1 tbsp za'atar
- salt
- TO GARNISH
- 2 green onions, thinly sliced
- 2 tbsp / 15 g toasted hazelnuts, coarsely crushed
- 2 oz / 60 g soft goat's milk cheese, crumbled

INSTRUCTIONS

a) Preheat the oven to 400°F / 200°C.

b) Wash the beets and place in a roasting pan. Put them in the oven and cook, uncovered, until a knife slides easily into the center, about 1 hour. Once they are cool enough to handle, peel the beets and cut each one into about 6 pieces. Allow to cool down.

c) Place the beets, garlic, chile, and yogurt in a food processor and blend to a smooth paste. Transfer to a large mixing bowl and stir in the date syrup, olive oil, za'atar, and 1 teaspoon salt. Taste and add more salt if you like.

d) Transfer the mixture to a flat serving plate and use the back of a spoon to spread it around the plate. Scatter the green onions, hazelnuts, and cheese on top and finally drizzle with a bit of oil. Serve at room temperature.

27. Swiss chard fritters

Makes: 4 AS A STARTER

INGREDIENTS
- 14 oz / 400 g Swiss chard leaves, white stalks removed
- 1 oz / 30 g flat-leaf parsley
- ⅔ oz / 20 g cilantro
- ⅔ oz / 20 g dill
- 1½ tsp grated nutmeg
- ½ tsp sugar
- 3 tbsp all-purpose flour
- 2 cloves garlic, crushed
- 2 large free-range eggs
- 3 oz / 80 g feta cheese, broken into small pieces
- 4 tbsp / 60 ml olive oil
- 1 lemon, cut into 4 wedges
- salt and freshly ground black pepper

INSTRUCTIONS
a) Bring a large pan of salted water to a boil, add the chard, and simmer for 5 minutes. Drain the leaves and squeeze them well until completely dry. Place in a food processor along with the herbs, nutmeg, sugar, flour, garlic, eggs, generous ¼ teaspoon salt, and some black pepper. Blitz until smooth and then fold the feta through the mix by hand.

b) Pour 1 tablespoon of the oil into a medium frying pan. Place over medium-high heat and spoon in a heaping tablespoon of mixture for each fritter. Press down gently to get a fritter 2¾ inches / 7 cm wide and ⅜ inch / 1 cm thick. You should be able to fit about 3 fritters at a time. Cook the fritters for 3 to 4 minutes in total, turning once, until they have taken on some color.

c) Transfer to paper towels, then keep each batch warm while you cook the remaining mixture, adding the remaining oil as needed. Serve at once with the lemon wedges.

28. Spiced Chickpeas & Vegetable Salad

Makes: 4

INGREDIENTS
- ½ cup / 100 g dried chickpeas
- 1 tsp baking soda
- 2 small cucumbers (10 oz / 280 g in total)
- 2 large tomatoes (10½ oz / 300 g in total)
- 8½ oz / 240 g radishes
- 1 red pepper, seeded and ribs removed
- 1 small red onion, peeled
- ⅔ oz / 20 g cilantro leaves and stems, coarsely chopped
- ½ oz / 15 g flat-leaf parsley, coarsely chopped
- 6 tbsp / 90 ml olive oil
- grated zest of 1 lemon, plus 2 tbsp juice
- 1½ tbsp sherry vinegar
- 1 clove garlic, crushed
- 1 tsp superfine sugar
- 1 tsp ground cardamom
- 1½ tsp ground allspice
- 1 tsp ground cumin
- Greek yogurt (optional)
- salt and freshly ground black pepper

INSTRUCTIONS

a) Soak the dried chickpeas overnight in a large bowl with plenty of cold water and the baking soda. The next day, drain, place in a large saucepan, and cover with water twice the volume of the chickpeas. Bring to a boil and simmer, skimming off any foam, for about an hour, until completely tender, then drain.

b) Cut the cucumber, tomato, radish, and pepper into ⅔-inch / 1.5cm dice; cut the onion into ¼-inch / 0.5cm dice. Mix everything together in a bowl with the cilantro and parsley.

c) In a jar or sealable container, mix 5 tbsp / 75 ml of the olive oil, the lemon juice and zest, vinegar, garlic, and sugar and mix well to form a dressing, then season to taste with salt and pepper. Pour the dressing over the salad and toss lightly.

d) Mix together the cardamom, allspice, cumin, and ¼ teaspoon salt and spread on a plate. Toss the cooked chickpeas in the spice mixture in a few batches to coat well. Heat the remaining olive oil in a frying pan over medium heat and lightly fry the chickpeas for 2 to 3 minutes, gently shaking the pan so they cook evenly and don't stick. Keep warm.

e) Divide the salad among four plates, arranging it in a large circle, and spoon the warm spiced chickpeas on top, keeping the edge of the salad clear. You can drizzle some Greek yogurt on top to make the salad creamy.

29. Chermoula Eggplant with Bulgur & Yogurt

Makes: 4 AS A MAIN COURSE

INGREDIENTS
- 2 cloves garlic, crushed
- 2 tsp ground cumin
- 2 tsp ground coriander
- 1 tsp chile flakes
- 1 tsp sweet paprika
- 2 tbsp finely chopped preserved lemon peel (store-bought or see recipe)
- ⅔ cup / 140 ml olive oil, plus extra to finish
- 2 medium eggplants
- 1 cup / 150 g fine bulgur
- ⅔ cup / 140 ml boiling water
- ⅓ cup / 50 g golden raisins
- 3½ tbsp / 50 ml warm water
- ⅓ oz / 10 g cilantro, chopped, plus extra to finish
- ⅓ oz / 10 g mint, chopped
- ⅓ cup / 50 g pitted green olives, halved
- ⅓ cup / 30 g sliced almonds, toasted
- 3 green onions, chopped
- 1½ tbsp freshly squeezed lemon juice
- ½ cup / 120 g Greek yogurt
- salt

INSTRUCTIONS
a) Preheat the oven to 400°F / 200°C.
b) To make the chermoula, mix together in a small bowl the garlic, cumin, coriander, chile, paprika, preserved lemon, two-thirds of the olive oil, and ½ teaspoon salt.
c) Cut the eggplants in half lengthwise. Score the flesh of each half with deep, diagonal crisscross scores, making sure not to pierce the skin. Spoon the chermoula over each half, spreading it evenly, and place on a baking sheet cut side up. Put in the oven

and roast for 40 minutes, or until the eggplants are completely soft.
d) Meanwhile, place the bulgur in a large bowl and cover with the boiling water.
e) Soak the raisins in the warm water. After 10 minutes, drain the raisins and add them to the bulgur, along with the remaining oil. Add the herbs, olives, almonds, green onions, lemon juice, and a pinch of salt and stir to combine. Taste and add more salt if necessary.
f) Serve the eggplants warm or at room temperature. Place ½ eggplant, cut side up, on each individual plate. Spoon the bulgur on top, allowing some to fall from both sides. Spoon over some yogurt, sprinkle with cilantro, and finish with a drizzle of oil.

30. Fried cauliflower with tahini

Makes: 6

INGREDIENTS
- 2 cups / 500 ml sunflower oil
- 2 medium heads cauliflower (2¼ lb / 1 kg in total), divided into small florets
- 8 green onions, each divided into 3 long segments
- ¾ cup / 180 g light tahini paste
- 2 cloves garlic, crushed
- ¼ cup / 15 g flat-leaf parsley, chopped
- ¼ cup / 15 g chopped mint, plus extra to finish
- ⅔ cup / 150 g Greek yogurt
- ¼ cup / 60ml freshly squeezed lemon juice, plus grated zest of 1 lemon
- 1 tsp pomegranate molasses, plus extra to finish
- about ¾ cup / 180 ml water
- Maldon sea salt and freshly ground black pepper

INSTRUCTIONS

a) Heat the sunflower oil in a large saucepan placed over medium-high heat. Using a pair of metal tongs or a metal spoon, carefully place a few cauliflower florets at a time into the oil and cook them for 2 to 3 minutes, turning them over so they color evenly. Once golden brown, use a slotted spoon to lift the florets into a colander to drain. Sprinkle with a little salt. Continue in batches until you finish all the cauliflower. Next, fry the green onions in batches but for only about 1 minute. Add to the cauliflower. Allow both to cool down a little.

b) Pour the tahini paste into a large mixing bowl and add the garlic, chopped herbs, yogurt, lemon juice and zest, pomegranate molasses, and some salt and pepper. Stir well with a wooden spoon as you add the water. The tahini sauce will thicken and then loosen up as you add water. Don't add too much, just enough to get a thick, yet smooth, pourable consistency, a bit like honey.

c) Add the cauliflower and green onions to the tahini and stir well. Taste and adjust the seasoning. You may also want to add more lemon juice.

d) To serve, spoon into a serving bowl and finish with a few drops of pomegranate molasses and some mint.

31. Roasted Cauliflower & Hazelnut Salad

Makes: 2 TO 4

INGREDIENTS
- 1 head cauliflower, broken into small florets (1½ lb / 660 g in total)
- 5 tbsp olive oil
- 1 large celery stalk, cut on an angle into ¼-inch / 0.5cm slices (⅔ cup / 70 g in total)
- 5 tbsp / 30 g hazelnuts, with skins
- ⅓ cup / 10 g small flat-leaf parsley leaves, picked
- ⅓ cup / 50 g pomegranate seeds (from about ½ medium pomegranate)
- generous ¼ tsp ground cinnamon
- generous ¼ tsp ground allspice
- 1 tbsp sherry vinegar
- 1½ tsp maple syrup
- salt and freshly ground black pepper

INSTRUCTIONS
a) Preheat the oven to 425°F / 220°C.
b) Mix the cauliflower with 3 tablespoons of the olive oil, ½ teaspoon salt, and some black pepper. Spread out in a roasting pan and roast on the top oven rack for 25 to 35 minutes, until the cauliflower is crisp and parts of it have turned golden brown. Transfer to a large mixing bowl and set aside to cool down.
c) Decrease the oven temperature to 325°F / 170°C. Spread the hazelnuts on a baking sheet lined with parchment paper and roast for 17 minutes.
d) Allow the nuts to cool a little, then coarsely chop them and add to the cauliflower, along with the remaining oil and the rest of the ingredients. Stir, taste, and season with salt and pepper accordingly. Serve at room temperature.

32. A'ja (bread fritters)

Makes: ABOUT 8 FRITTERS

INGREDIENTS
- 4 white bread slices, crusts removed (3 oz / 80 g in total)
- 4 extra-large free-range eggs
- 1½ tsp ground cumin
- ½ tsp sweet paprika
- ¼ tsp cayenne pepper
- 1 oz / 25 g chives, chopped
- 1 oz / 25 g flat-leaf parsley, chopped
- ⅓ oz / 10 g tarragon, chopped
- 1½ oz / 40 g feta cheese, crumbled
- sunflower oil, for frying
- salt and freshly ground black pepper

INSTRUCTIONS
a) Soak the bread in plenty of cold water for 1 minute, then squeeze well.
b) Crumble the soaked bread into a medium bowl, then add the eggs, spices, ½ teaspoon salt, and ¼ teaspoon pepper and whisk well. Mix in the chopped herbs and feta.
c) Heat 1 tablespoon oil in a medium frying pan over medium-high heat. Spoon about 3 tablespoons of the mixture into the center of the pan for each fritter and flatten it using the underside of the spoon; the fritters should be ¾ to 1¼ inches / 2 to 3 cm thick. Fry the fritters for 2 to 3 minutes on each side, until golden brown. Repeat with the remaining batter. You should get about 8 fritters.
d) Alternatively, you can fry all the batter at once, as you would a large omelet. Slice and serve warm or at room temperature.

33. Spicy carrot salad

Makes: 4

INGREDIENTS
- 6 large carrots, peeled (about 1½ lb / 700 g in total)
- 3 tbsp sunflower oil
- 1 large onion, finely chopped (2 cups / 300 g in total)
- 1 tbsp Pilpelchuma or 2 tbsp harissa (store-bought or see recipe)
- ½ tsp ground cumin
- ½ tsp caraway seeds, freshly ground
- ½ tsp sugar
- 3 tbsp cider vinegar
- 1½ cups / 30 g arugula leaves
- salt

INSTRUCTIONS
a) Place the carrots in a large saucepan, cover with water, and bring to a boil. Decrease the heat, cover, and cook for about 20 minutes, until the carrots are just tender. Drain and, once cool enough to handle, cut into ¼-inch / 0.5cm slices.
b) While the carrots are cooking, heat half the oil in a large frying pan. Add the onion and cook over medium heat for 10 minutes, until golden brown.
c) Tip the fried onion into a large mixing bowl and add the pilpelchuma, cumin, caraway, ¾ teaspoon salt, sugar, vinegar, and the remaining oil. Add the carrots and toss well. Leave aside for at least 30 minutes for the flavors to mature.
d) Arrange the salad on a large platter, dotting with the arugula as you go.

34. <u>Hannukah</u> Shakshuka

Makes: 2 TO 4

INGREDIENTS
- 2 tbsp olive oil
- 2 tbsp Pilpelchuma or harissa (store-bought or see recipe)
- 2 tsp tomato paste
- 2 large red peppers, cut into ¼-inch / 0.5cm dice (2 cups / 300 g in total)
- 4 cloves garlic, finely chopped
- 1 tsp ground cumin
- 5 large, very ripe tomatoes, chopped (5 cups / 800 g in total); canned are also fine
- 4 large free-range eggs, plus 4 egg yolks
- ½ cup / 120 g labneh (store-bought or see recipe) or thick yogurt
- salt

INSTRUCTIONS

a) Heat the olive oil in a large frying pan over medium heat and add the pilpelchuma or harissa, tomato paste, peppers, garlic, cumin, and ¾ teaspoon salt. Stir and cook over medium heat for about 8 minutes to allow the peppers to soften. Add the tomatoes, bring to a gentle simmer, and cook for a further 10 minutes until you have quite a thick sauce. Taste for seasoning.

b) Make 8 little dips in the sauce. Gently break the eggs and carefully pour each into its own dip. Do the same with the yolks. Use a fork to swirl the egg whites a little bit with the sauce, taking care not to break the yolks. Simmer gently for 8 to 10 minutes, until the egg whites are set but the yolks are still runny (you can cover the pan with a lid if you wish to hasten the process).

c) Remove from the heat, leave for a couple of minutes to settle, then spoon into individual plates and serve with the labneh or yogurt.

35. Butternut Squash & Tahini Spread

Makes: 6 TO 8

INGREDIENTS
- 1 very large butternut squash (about 2½ lb / 1.2 kg), peeled and cut into chunks (7 cups / 970 g in total)
- 3 tbsp olive oil
- 1 tsp ground cinnamon
- 5 tbsp / 70 g light tahini paste
- ½ cup / 120 g Greek yogurt
- 2 small cloves garlic, crushed
- 1 tsp mixed black and white sesame seeds (or just white, if you don't have black)
- 1½ tsp date syrup
- 2 tbsp chopped cilantro (optional)
- salt

INSTRUCTIONS
a) Preheat the oven to 400°F / 200°C.
b) Spread the squash out in a medium roasting pan. Pour over the olive oil and sprinkle on the cinnamon and ½ teaspoon salt. Mix together well, cover the pan tightly with aluminum foil, and roast in the oven for 70 minutes, stirring once during the cooking. Remove from the oven and leave to cool.
c) Transfer the squash to a food processor, along with the tahini, yogurt, and garlic. Roughly pulse so that everything is combined into a coarse paste, without the spread becoming smooth; you can also do this by hand using a fork or potato masher.
d) Spread the butternut in a wavy pattern over a flat plate and sprinkle with the sesame seeds, drizzle over the syrup, and finish with the cilantro, if using.

36. Spicy Beet, Leek & Walnut Salad

INGREDIENTS

- 4 medium beets (⅓ lb / 600 g in total after cooking and peeling)
- 4 medium leeks, cut into 4-inch / 10cm segments (4 cups / 360 g in total)
- ½ oz / 15 g cilantro, coarsely chopped
- 1¼ cups / 25 g arugula
- ⅓ cup / 50 g pomegranate seeds (optional)
- **DRESSING**
- 1 cup / 100 g walnuts, coarsely chopped
- 4 cloves garlic, finely chopped
- ½ tsp chile flakes
- ¼ cup / 60 ml cider vinegar
- 2 tbsp tamarind water
- ½ tsp walnut oil
- 2½ tbsp peanut oil
- 1 tsp salt

INSTRUCTIONS

a) Preheat the oven to 425°F / 220°C.

b) Wrap the beets individually in aluminum foil and roast them in the oven for 1 to 1½ hours, depending on their size. Once cooked, you should be able to stick a small knife through to the center easily. Remove from the oven and set aside to cool.

c) Once cool enough to handle, peel the beets, halve them, and cut each half into wedges ⅜ inch / 1 cm thick at the base. Put in a medium bowl and set aside.

d) Place the leeks in a medium pan with salted water, bring to a boil, and simmer for 10 minutes, until just cooked; it's important to simmer them gently and not to overcook them so they don't fall apart. Drain and refresh under cold water, then use a very sharp serrated knife to cut each segment into 3 smaller pieces and pat dry. Transfer to a bowl, separate from the beets, and set aside.

e) While the vegetables are cooking, mix together all the dressing ingredients and leave to one side for at least 10 minutes for all the flavors to come together.

f) Divide the walnut dressing and the cilantro equally between the beets and the leeks and toss gently. Taste both and add more salt if needed.

g) To put the salad together, spread most of the beets on a serving platter, top with some arugula, then most of the leeks, then the remaining beets, and finish with more leeks and arugula. Sprinkle over the pomegranate seeds, if using, and serve.

37.　Charred Okra with Tomato

Makes: 2 AS A SIDE DISH

INGREDIENTS
- 10½ oz / 300 g baby or very small okra
- 2 tbsp olive oil, plus more if needed
- 4 cloves garlic, thinly sliced
- ⅔ oz / 20 g preserved lemon peel (store-bought or see recipe), cut into ⅜-inch / 1cm wedges
- 3 small tomatoes (7 oz / 200 g in total), cut into 8 wedges, or halved cherry tomatoes
- 1½ tsp chopped flat-leaf parsley
- 1½ tsp chopped cilantro
- 1 tbsp freshly squeezed lemon juice
- Maldon sea salt and freshly ground black pepper

INSTRUCTIONS
a) Using a small, sharp fruit knife, trim the okra pods, removing the stem just above the pod so as not to expose the seeds.

b) Place a large, heavy-bottomed frying pan over high heat and leave for a few minutes. When almost red hot, throw in the okra in two batches and dry-cook, shaking the pan occasionally, for 4 minutes per batch. The okra pods should have the occasional dark blister.

c) Return all the charred okra to the pan and add the olive oil, garlic, and preserved lemon. Stir-fry for 2 minutes, shaking the pan. Reduce the heat to medium and add the tomatoes, 2 tablespoons water, the chopped herbs, lemon juice, and ½ teaspoon salt and some black pepper. Stir everything together gently, so that the tomatoes do not break up, and continue to cook for 2 to 3 minutes, until the tomatoes are warmed through. Transfer to a serving dish, drizzle with more olive oil, add a sprinkle of salt, and serve.

38. Burnt Eggplant with Pomegranate Seeds

Makes: 4 AS PART OF A MEZE PLATE

INGREDIENTS
- 4 large eggplants (3¼ lb / 1.5 kg before cooking; 2½ cups / 550 g after burning and draining the flesh)
- 2 cloves garlic, crushed
- grated zest of 1 lemon and 2 tbsp freshly squeezed lemon juice
- 5 tbsp olive oil
- 2 tbsp chopped flat-leaf parsley
- 2 tbsp chopped mint
- seeds of ½ large pomegranate (½ cup / 80 g in total)
- salt and freshly ground black pepper

INSTRUCTIONS

a) If you have a gas range, line the base with aluminum foil to protect it, keeping only the burners exposed. Place the eggplants directly on four separate gas burners with medium flames and roast for 15 to 18 minutes, until the skin is burnt and flaky and the flesh is soft. Use metal tongs to turn them around occasionally. Alternatively, score the eggplants with a knife in a few places, about ¾ inch / 2 cm deep, and place on a baking sheet under a hot broiler for about an hour. Turn them around every 20 minutes or so and continue to cook even if they burst and break.

b) Remove the eggplants from the heat and allow them to cool down slightly. Once cool enough to handle, cut an opening along each eggplant and scoop out the soft flesh, dividing it with your hands into long thin strips. Discard the skin. Drain the flesh in a colander for at least an hour, preferably longer, to get rid of as much water as possible.

c) Place the eggplant pulp in a medium bowl and add the garlic, lemon zest and juice, olive oil, ½ teaspoon salt, and a good grind of black pepper. Stir and allow the eggplant to marinate at room temperature for at least an hour.

d) When you are ready to serve, mix in most of the herbs and taste for seasoning. Pile high on a serving plate, scatter on the pomegranate seeds, and garnish with the remaining herbs.

39. Parsley & Barley Salad

Makes: 4

INGREDIENTS
- ¼ cup / 40 g pearl barley
- 5 oz / 150 g feta cheese
- 5½ tbsp olive oil
- 1 tsp za'atar
- ½ tsp coriander seeds, lightly toasted and crushed
- ¼ tsp ground cumin
- 3 oz / 80 g flat-leaf parsley, leaves and fine stems
- 4 green onions, finely chopped (⅓ cup / 40 g in total)
- 2 cloves garlic, crushed
- ⅓ cup / 40 g cashew nuts, lightly toasted and coarsely crushed
- 1 green pepper, seeded and cut into ⅜-inch / 1cm dice
- ½ tsp ground allspice
- 2 tbsp freshly squeezed lemon juice
- salt and freshly ground black pepper

INSTRUCTIONS
a) Place the pearl barley in a small saucepan, cover with plenty of water, and boil for 30 to 35 minutes, until tender but with a bite. Pour into a fine sieve, shake to remove all the water, and transfer to a large bowl.

b) Break the feta into rough pieces, about ¾ inch / 2 cm in size, and mix in a small bowl with 1½ tablespoons of the olive oil, the za'atar, the coriander seeds, and the cumin. Gently mix together and leave to marinate while you prepare the rest of the salad.

c) Chop the parsley finely and place in a bowl with the green onions, garlic, cashew nuts, pepper, allspice, lemon juice, the remaining olive oil, and the cooked barley. Mix together well and season to taste. To serve, divide the salad among four plates and top with the marinated feta.

40. Chunky zucchini & tomato salad

Makes: 6

INGREDIENTS
- 8 pale green zucchini or regular zucchini (about 2¼ lb / 1 kg in total)
- 5 large, very ripe tomatoes (1¾ lb / 800 g in total)
- 3 tbsp olive oil, plus extra to finish
- 2½ cups / 300 g Greek yogurt
- 2 cloves garlic, crushed
- 2 red chiles, seeded and chopped
- grated zest of 1 medium lemon and 2 tbsp freshly squeezed lemon juice
- 1 tbsp date syrup, plus extra to finish
- 2 cups / 200 g walnuts, coarsely chopped
- 2 tbsp chopped mint
- ⅔ oz / 20 g flat-leaf parsley, chopped
- salt and freshly ground black pepper

INSTRUCTIONS

a) Preheat the oven to 425°F / 220°C. Place a ridged griddle pan over high heat.
b) Trim the zucchini and cut them in half lengthwise. Halve the tomatoes as well. Brush the zucchini and tomatoes with olive oil on the cut side and season with salt and pepper.
c) By now the griddle pan should be piping hot. Start with the zucchini. Place a few of them on the pan, cut side down, and cook for 5 minutes; the zucchini should be nicely charred on one side. Now remove the zucchini and repeat the same process with the tomatoes. Place the vegetables in a roasting pan and put in the oven for about 20 minutes, until the zucchini are very tender.
d) Remove the pan from the oven and allow the vegetables to cool down slightly. Chop them coarsely and leave to drain in a colander for 15 minutes.
e) Whisk together the yogurt, garlic, chile, lemon zest and juice, and molasses in a large mixing bowl. Add the chopped vegetables, walnuts, mint, and most of the parsley and stir well. Season with ¾ teaspoon salt and some pepper.
f) Transfer the salad to a large, shallow serving plate and spread it out. Garnish with the remaining parsley. Finally, drizzle over some date syrup and olive oil.

41. Tabbouleh

Makes: 4 GENEROUSLY

INGREDIENTS
- ½ cup / 30 g fine bulgur wheat
- 2 large tomatoes, ripe but firm (10½ oz / 300 g in total)
- 1 shallot, finely chopped (3 tbsp / 30 g in total)
- 3 tbsp freshly squeezed lemon juice, plus a little extra to finish
- 4 large bunches flat-leaf parsley (5½ oz / 160 g in total)
- 2 bunches mint (1 oz / 30 g in total)
- 2 tsp ground allspice
- 1 tsp baharat spice mix (store-bought or see recipe)
- ½ cup / 80 ml top-quality olive oil
- seeds of about ½ large pomegranate (½ cup / 70 g in total), optional
- salt and freshly ground black pepper

INSTRUCTIONS

a) Put the bulgur in a fine sieve and run under cold water until the water coming through looks clear and most of the starch has been removed. Transfer to a large mixing bowl.

b) Use a small serrated knife to cut the tomatoes into slices ¼ inch / 0.5 cm thick. Cut each slice into ¼-inch / 0.5cm strips and then into dice. Add the tomatoes and their juices to the bowl, along with the shallot and lemon juice and stir well.

c) Take a few sprigs of parsley and pack them together tightly. Use a large, very sharp knife to trim off most of the stems and discard. Now use the knife to move up the stems and leaves, gradually "feeding" the knife in order to shred the parsley as finely as you can and trying to avoid cutting pieces wider than 1/16 inch / 1 mm. Add to the bowl.

d) Pick the mint leaves off the stems, pack a few together tightly, and shred them finely as you did the parsley; don't chop them up too much as they tend to discolor. Add to the bowl.

e) Finally, add the allspice, baharat, olive oil, pomegranate, if using, and some salt and pepper. Taste, and add more salt and pepper if you like, possibly a little bit of lemon juice, and serve.

42. Roasted potatoes with caramel & prunes

Makes: 4

INGREDIENTS
- 2¼ lb / 1 kg floury potatoes, such as russet
- ½ cup / 120 ml goose fat
- 5 oz / 150 g whole soft Agen prunes, pitted
- ½ cup / 90 g superfine sugar
- 3½ tbsp / 50 ml iced water
- salt

INSTRUCTIONS

a) Preheat the oven to 475°F / 240°C.

b) Peel the potatoes, leave the small ones whole and halve the larger ones, so you end up with pieces of around 2 oz / 60 g. Rinse under cold water, then place the potatoes in a large pan with plenty of fresh cold water. Bring to a boil, and simmer for 8 to 10 minutes. Drain the potatoes well, then shake the colander to roughen their edges.

c) Place the goose fat in a roasting pan and heat in the oven until smoking, about 8 minutes. Carefully take the pan out of the oven and add the boiled potatoes to the hot fat with metal tongs, rolling them around in the fat as you do so. Gently place the pan on the highest rack of the oven and cook for 50 to 65 minutes, or until the potatoes are golden and crunchy on the outside. Turn them over from time to time while they are cooking.

d) Once the potatoes are almost ready, take the tray out of the oven and tip it over a heatproof bowl to remove most of the fat. Add ½ teaspoon salt and the prunes and stir gently. Return to the oven for another 5 minutes.

e) During this time, make the caramel. Put the sugar in a clean, heavy-bottomed saucepan and place over low heat. Without stirring, watch the sugar turn a rich caramel color. Make sure to keep your eyes on the sugar at all times. As soon as you reach this color, remove the pan from the heat. Holding the pan at a safe distance from your face, quickly pour the iced water into the caramel to stop it from cooking. Return to the heat and stir to remove any sugar lumps.

f) Before serving, stir the caramel into the potatoes and prunes. Transfer to a serving bowl and eat at once.

43. Swiss Chard with Tahini, Yogurt & Buttered Pine Nuts

Makes: 4

INGREDIENTS
- 2¾ lb / 1.3 kg Swiss chard
- 2½ tbsp / 40 g unsalted butter
- 2 tbsp olive oil, plus extra to finish
- 5 tbsp / 40 g pine nuts
- 2 small cloves garlic, sliced very thinly
- ¼ cup / 60 ml dry white wine
- sweet paprika, to garnish (optional)
- salt and freshly ground black pepper

TAHINI & YOGURT SAUCE
- 3½ tbsp / 50 g light tahini paste
- 4½ tbsp / 50 g Greek yogurt
- 2 tbsp freshly squeezed lemon juice
- 1 clove garlic, crushed
- 2 tbsp water

INSTRUCTIONS

a) Start with the sauce. Place all the ingredients in a medium bowl, add a pinch of salt, and stir well with a small whisk until you get a smooth, semistiff paste. Set aside.

b) Use a sharp knife to separate the white chard stalks from the green leaves and cut both into slices ¾ inch / 2 cm wide, keeping them separate. Bring a large pan of salted water to a boil and add the chard stalks. Simmer for 2 minutes, add the leaves, and cook for a further minute. Drain and rinse well under cold water. Allow the water to drain and then use your hands to squeeze the chard until it is completely dry.

c) Put half the butter and the 2 tablespoons olive oil in a large frying pan and place over medium heat. Once hot, add the pine nuts and toss them in the pan until golden, about 2 minutes. Use a slotted spoon to remove them from the pan, then throw in the garlic. Cook for about a minute, until it starts to become golden. Carefully (it will spit!) pour in the wine. Leave for a minute or less, until it reduces to about one-third. Add the chard and the rest of the butter and cook for 2 to 3 minutes, stirring occasionally, until the chard is completely warm. Season with ½ teaspoon salt and some black pepper.

d) Divide the chard among individual serving bowls, spoon some tahini sauce on top, and scatter with the pine nuts. Finally, drizzle with olive oil and sprinkle with some paprika, if you like.

44. Hannukah Sabih

Makes: 4

INGREDIENTS
- 2 large eggplants (about 1⅔ lb / 750 g in total)
- about 1¼ cups / 300 ml sunflower oil
- 4 slices good-quality white bread, toasted, or fresh and moist mini pitas
- 1 cup / 240 ml Tahini sauce
- 4 large free-range eggs, hard-boiled, peeled, and cut into ⅜-inch / 1cm thick slices or quartered
- about 4 tbsp Zhoug
- amba or savory mango pickle (optional)
- salt and freshly ground black pepper

CHOPPED SALAD
- 2 medium ripe tomatoes, cut into ⅜-inch / 1cm dice (about 1 cup / 200 g in total)
- 2 mini cucumbers, cut into ⅜-inch / 1cm dice (about 1 cup / 120 g in total)
- 2 green onions, thinly sliced
- 1½ tbsp chopped flat-leaf parsley
- 2 tsp freshly squeezed lemon juice
- 1½ tbsp olive oil

INSTRUCTIONS

a) Use a vegetable peeler to peel away strips of eggplant skin from top to bottom, leaving the eggplants with alternating strips of black skin and white flesh, zebralike. Cut both eggplants widthwise into slices 1 inch / 2.5 cm thick. Sprinkle them on both sides with salt, then spread them out on a baking sheet and let stand for at least 30 minutes to remove some water. Use paper towels to wipe them.

b) Heat the sunflower oil in a wide frying pan. Carefully—the oil spits—fry the eggplant slices in batches until nice and dark, turning once, 6 to 8 minutes total. Add oil if needed as you cook the batches. When done, the eggplant pieces should be completely tender in the center. Remove from the pan and drain on paper towels.

c) Make the chopped salad by mixing together all the ingredients and seasoning with salt and pepper to taste.

d) Just before serving, place 1 slice of bread or pita on each plate. Spoon 1 tablespoon of the tahini sauce over each slice, then arrange the eggplant slices on top, overlapping. Drizzle over some more tahini but without completely covering the eggplant slices. Season each egg slice with salt and pepper and arrange over the eggplant. Drizzle some more tahini on top and spoon over as much zhoug as you like; be careful, it's hot! Spoon over mango pickle as well, if you like. Serve the vegetable salad on the side, spooning some on top of every serving if desired.

45. Latkes

Makes: 12 LATKES

INGREDIENTS
- 5½ cups / 600 g peeled and grated fairly waxy potatoes such as Yukon Gold
- 2¾ cups / 300 g peeled and grated parsnips
- ⅔ cup / 30 g chives, finely chopped
- 4 egg whites
- 2 tbsp cornstarch
- 5 tbsp / 80 g unsalted butter
- 6½ tbsp / 100 ml sunflower oil
- salt and freshly ground black pepper
- sour cream, to serve

INSTRUCTIONS

a) Rinse the potato in a large bowl of cold water. Drain in a colander, squeeze out any excess water, and then spread the potato out on a clean kitchen towel to dry completely.

b) In a large bowl, mix together the potato, parsnip, chives, egg whites, cornstarch, 1 teaspoon salt, and plenty of black pepper.

c)

d) Heat half the butter and half the oil in a large frying pan over medium-high heat. Use your hands to pick out portions of about 2 tablespoons of the latke mix, squeeze firmly to remove some of the liquid, and shape into thin patties about 3/8 inch / 1 cm thick and 3¼ inches / 8 cm in diameter. Carefully place as many latkes as you can comfortably fit in the pan, push them down gently, and level them with the back of a spoon. Fry over medium-high heat for 3 minutes on each side. The latkes need to be completely brown on the outside. Remove the fried latkes from the oil, place on paper towels, and keep warm while you cook the rest. Add the remaining butter and oil as needed. Serve at once with sour cream on the side.

46. **Hannukah** Falafel

Makes: ABOUT 20 BALLS

INGREDIENTS
- 1¼ cups / 250 g dried chickpeas
- ½ medium onion, finely chopped (½ cup / 80 g in total)
- 1 clove garlic, crushed
- 1 tbsp finely chopped flat-leaf parsley
- 2 tbsp finely chopped cilantro
- ¼ tsp cayenne pepper
- ½ tsp ground cumin
- ½ tsp ground coriander
- ¼ tsp ground cardamom
- ½ tsp baking powder
- 3 tbsp water
- 1½ tbsp all-purpose flour
- about 3 cups / 750 ml sunflower oil, for deep-frying
- ½ tsp sesame seeds, for coating
- salt

INSTRUCTIONS

a) Place the chickpeas in a large bowl and cover with cold water at least twice their volume. Set aside to soak overnight.

b) The next day, drain the chickpeas well and combine them with the onion, garlic, parsley, and cilantro. For the best results, use a meat grinder for the next part. Put the chickpea mixture once through the machine, set to its finest setting, then pass it through the machine for a second time. If you don't have a meat grinder, use a food processor. Blitz the mix in batches, pulsing each for 30 to 40 seconds, until it is finely chopped, but not mushy or pasty, and holds itself together. Once processed, add the spices, baking powder, ¾ teaspoon salt, flour, and water. Mix well by hand until smooth and uniform. Cover the mixture and leave it in the fridge for at least 1 hour, or until ready to use.

c) Fill a deep, heavy-bottomed medium saucepan with enough oil to come 2¾ inches / 7 cm up the sides of the pan. Heat the oil to 350°F / 180°C.
d) With wet hands, press 1 tablespoon of the mixture in the palm of your hand to form a patty or a ball the size of a small walnut, about a 1 oz / 25 g (you can also use a wet ice-cream scoop for this).
e) Sprinkle the balls evenly with sesame seeds and deep-fry them in batches for 4 minutes, until well browned and cooked through. It is important they really dry out on the inside, so make sure they get enough time in the oil. Drain in a colander lined with paper towels and serve at once.

47. Wheat Berries & Swiss Chard with Pomegranate Molasses

Makes: 4

INGREDIENTS
- 1⅓ lb / 600 g Swiss chard or rainbow chard
- 2 tbsp olive oil
- 1 tbsp unsalted butter
- 2 large leeks, white and pale green parts, thinly sliced (3 cups / 350 g in total)
- 2 tbsp light brown sugar
- about 3 tbsp pomegranate molasses
- 1¼ cups / 200 g hulled or unhulled wheat berries
- 2 cups / 500 ml chicken stock
- salt and freshly ground black pepper
- Greek yogurt, to serve

INSTRUCTIONS
a) Separate the chard's white stalks from the green leaves using a small, sharp knife. Slice the stalks into ⅜-inch / 1cm slices and the leaves into ¾-inch / 2cm slices.
b) Heat the oil and butter in a large heavy-bottomed pan. Add the leeks and cook, stirring, for 3 to 4 minutes. Add the chard stalks and cook for 3 minutes, then add the leaves and cook for a further 3 minutes. Add the sugar, 3 tablespoons pomegranate molasses, and the wheat berries and mix well. Add the stock, ¾ teaspoon salt, and some black pepper, bring to a gentle simmer, and cook over low heat, covered, for 60 to 70 minutes. The wheat should be al dente at this point.
c) Remove the lid and, if needed, increase the heat and allow any remaining liquid to evaporate. The base of the pan should be dry and have a bit of burnt caramel on it. Remove from the heat.
d) Before serving, taste and add more molasses, salt, and pepper if needed; you want it sharp and sweet, so don't be shy with your molasses. Serve warm, with a dollop of Greek yogurt.

48. Hannukah Balilah

Makes: 4

INGREDIENTS
- 1 cup / 200 g dried chickpeas
- 1 tsp baking soda
- 1 cup / 60 g chopped flat-leaf parsley
- 2 green onions, thinly sliced
- 1 large lemon
- 3 tbsp olive oil
- 2½ tsp ground cumin
- salt and freshly ground black pepper

INSTRUCTIONS

a) The night before, put the chickpeas in a large bowl and cover with cold water at least twice their volume. Add the baking soda and leave at room temperature to soak overnight.

b) Drain the chickpeas and place them in a large saucepan. Cover with plenty of cold water and place over high heat. Bring to a boil, skim the surface of the water, then decrease the heat and simmer for 1 to 1½ hours, until the chickpeas are very soft but still retain their shape.

c) While the chickpeas are cooking, put the parsley and green onions in a large mixing bowl. Peel the lemon by topping and tailing it, placing on a board, and running a small sharp knife along its curves to remove the skin and white pith. Discard the skin, pith, and seeds and coarsely chop the flesh. Add the flesh and all of the juices to the bowl.

d) Once the chickpeas are ready, drain and add them to the bowl while they are still hot. Add the olive oil, cumin, ¾ teaspoon salt, and a good grind of pepper. Mix well. Allow to cool down until just warm, taste for seasoning, and serve.

49. Basmati rice & orzo

Makes: 6

INGREDIENTS
- 1⅓ cups / 250 g basmati rice
- 1 tbsp melted ghee or unsalted butter
- 1 tbsp sunflower oil
- ½ cup / 85 g orzo
- 2½ cups / 600 ml chicken stock
- 1 tsp salt

INSTRUCTIONS
a) Wash the basmati rice well, then place in a large bowl and cover with plenty of cold water. Allow it to soak for 30 minutes, then drain.

b) Heat the ghee and oil over medium-high heat in a medium heavy-bottomed saucepan for which you have a lid. Add the orzo and sauté for 3 to 4 minutes, until the grains turn dark golden. Add the stock, bring to a boil, and cook for 3 minutes. Add the drained rice and salt, bring to a gentle boil, stir once or twice, cover the pan, and simmer over very low heat for 15 minutes. Don't be tempted to uncover the pan; you'll need to allow the rice to steam properly.

c) Turn off the heat, remove the lid, and quickly cover the pan with a clean tea towel. Place the lid back on top of the towel and leave for 10 minutes. Fluff the rice with a fork before serving.

50. Saffron Rice with Barberries, Pistachio & Mixed Herbs

Makes: 6

INGREDIENTS
- 2½ tbsp / 40 g unsalted butter
- 2 cups / 360 g basmati rice, rinsed under cold water and drained well
- 2⅓ cups / 560 ml boiling water
- 1 tsp saffron threads, soaked in 3 tbsp boiling water for 30 minutes
- ¼ cup / 40 g dried barberries, soaked for a few minutes in boiling water with a pinch of sugar
- 1 oz / 30 g dill, coarsely chopped
- ⅔ oz / 20 g chervil, coarsely chopped
- ⅓ oz / 10 g tarragon, coarsely chopped
- ½ cup / 60 g slivered or crushed unsalted pistachios, lightly toasted
- salt and freshly ground white pepper

INSTRUCTIONS

a) Melt the butter in a medium saucepan and stir in the rice, making sure the grains are well coated in butter. Add the boiling water, 1 teaspoon salt, and some white pepper. Mix well, cover with a tightly fitting lid, and leave to cook over very low heat for 15 minutes. Don't be tempted to uncover the pan; you'll need to allow the rice to steam properly.

b) Remove the rice pan from the heat—all the water will have been absorbed by the rice—and pour the saffron water over one side of the rice, covering about one-quarter of the surface and leaving the majority of it white. Cover the pan immediately with a tea towel and reseal tightly with the lid. Set aside for 5 to 10 minutes.

c) Use a large spoon to remove the white part of the rice into a large mixing bowl and fluff it up with a fork. Drain the barberries and stir them in, followed by the herbs and most of the pistachios, leaving a few to garnish. Mix well. Fluff the saffron rice with a fork and gently fold it into the white rice. Don't overmix—you don't want the white grains to be stained by the yellow. Taste and adjust the seasoning. Transfer the rice to a shallow serving bowl and scatter the remaining pistachios on top. Serve warm or at room temperature.

51. Basmati & Wild Rice with Chickpeas, Currants & Herbs

Makes: 6

INGREDIENTS
- ⅓ cup / 50 g wild rice
- 2½ tbsp olive oil
- rounded 1 cup / 220 g basmati rice
- 1½ cups / 330 ml boiling water
- 2 tsp cumin seeds
- 1½ tsp curry powder
- 1½ cups / 240 g cooked and drained chickpeas (canned are fine)
- ¾ cup / 180 ml sunflower oil
- 1 medium onion, thinly sliced
- 1½ tsp all-purpose flour
- ⅔ cup / 100 g currants
- 2 tbsp chopped flat-leaf parsley
- 1 tbsp chopped cilantro
- 1 tbsp chopped dill
- salt and freshly ground black pepper

INSTRUCTIONS

a) Start by putting the wild rice in a small saucepan, cover with plenty of water, bring to a boil, and leave to simmer for about 40 minutes, until the rice is cooked but still quite firm. Drain and set aside.

b) To cook the basmati rice, pour 1 tablespoon of the olive oil into a medium saucepan with a tightly fitting lid and place over high heat. Add the rice and ¼ teaspoon salt and stir as you warm up the rice. Carefully add the boiling water, decrease the heat to very low, cover the pan with the lid, and leave to cook for 15 minutes.

c) Remove the pan from the heat, cover with a clean tea towel and then the lid, and leave off the heat for 10 minutes.

d) While the rice is cooking, prepare the chickpeas. Heat the remaining 1½ tbsp olive oil in a small saucepan over high heat. Add the cumin seeds and curry powder, wait for a couple seconds, and then add the chickpeas and ¼ teaspoon salt; make sure you do this quickly or the spices may burn in the oil. Stir over the heat for a minute or two, just to heat the chickpeas, then transfer to a large mixing bowl.

e) Wipe the saucepan clean, pour in the sunflower oil, and place over high heat. Make sure the oil is hot by throwing in a small piece of onion; it should sizzle vigorously. Use your hands to mix the onion with the flour to coat it slightly. Take some of the onion and carefully (it may spit!) place it in the oil. Fry for 2 to 3 minutes, until golden brown, then transfer to paper towels to drain and sprinkle with salt. Repeat in batches until all the onion is fried.

f) Finally, add both types of rice to the chickpeas and then add the currants, herbs, and fried onion. Stir, taste, and add salt and pepper as you like. Serve warm or at room temperature.

52. Barley Risotto with Marinated Feta

Makes: 4

INGREDIENTS
- 1 cup / 200 g pearl barley
- 2 tbsp / 30 g unsalted butter
- 6 tbsp / 90 ml olive oil
- 2 small celery stalks, cut into ¼-inch / 0.5cm dice
- 2 small shallots, cut into ¼-inch / 0.5cm dice
- 4 cloves garlic, cut into 1/16-inch / 2mm dice
- 4 thyme sprigs
- ½ tsp smoked paprika
- 1 bay leaf
- 4 strips lemon peel
- ¼ tsp chile flakes
- one 14-oz / 400g can chopped tomatoes
- 3 cups / 700 ml vegetable stock
- 1¼ cups / 300 ml passata (sieved crushed tomatoes)
- 1 tbsp caraway seeds
- 10½ oz / 300 g feta cheese, broken into roughly ¾-inch / 2cm pieces
- 1 tbsp fresh oregano leaves
- salt

INSTRUCTIONS
a) Rinse the pearl barley well under cold water and leave to drain.
b) Melt the butter and 2 tablespoons of the olive oil in a very large frying pan and cook the celery, shallots, and garlic over gentle heat for 5 minutes, until soft. Add the barley, thyme, paprika, bay leaf, lemon peel, chile flakes, tomatoes, stock, passata, and salt. Stir to combine. Bring the mixture to a boil, then reduce to a very gentle simmer and cook for 45 minutes, stirring frequently to make sure the risotto does not catch on the bottom of the pan. When ready, the barley should be tender and most of the liquid absorbed.

c) Meanwhile, toast the caraway seeds in a dry pan for a couple of minutes. Then lightly crush them so that some whole seeds remain. Add them to the feta with the remaining 4 tablespoons / 60 ml olive oil and gently mix to combine.
d) Once the risotto is ready, check the seasoning and then divide it among four shallow bowls. Top each with the marinated feta, including the oil, and a sprinkling of oregano leaves.

53. Conchiglie with Yogurt, Peas & Chile

Makes: 6

INGREDIENTS
- 2½ cups / 500 g Greek yogurt
- ⅔ cup / 150 ml olive oil
- 4 cloves garlic, crushed
- 1 lb / 500 g fresh or thawed frozen peas
- 1 lb / 500 g conchiglie pasta
- ½ cup / 60 g pine nuts
- 2 tsp Turkish or Syrian chile flakes (or less, depending on how spicy they are)
- 1⅔ cups / 40 g basil leaves, coarsely torn
- 8 oz / 240 g feta cheese, broken into chunks
- salt and freshly ground white pepper

INSTRUCTIONS

a) Put the yogurt, 6 tablespoons / 90 ml of the olive oil, the garlic, and ⅔ cup / 100 g of the peas in a food processor. Blitz to a uniform pale green sauce and transfer to a large mixing bowl.

b) Cook the pasta in plenty of salted boiling water until al dente. As the pasta cooks, heat the remaining olive oil in a small frying pan over medium heat. Add the pine nuts and chile flakes and fry for 4 minutes, until the nuts are golden and the oil is deep red. Also, heat the remaining peas in some boiling water, then drain.

c) Drain the cooked pasta into a colander, shake well to get rid of the water, and add the pasta gradually to the yogurt sauce; adding it all at once may cause the yogurt to split. Add the warm peas, basil, feta, 1 teaspoon salt, and ½ teaspoon white pepper. Toss gently, transfer to individual bowls, and spoon over the pine nuts and their oil.

54. Mejadra

Makes: 6

INGREDIENTS
- 1¼ cups / 250 g green or brown lentils
- 4 medium onions (1½ lb / 700 g before peeling)
- 3 tbsp all-purpose flour
- about 1 cup / 250 ml sunflower oil
- 2 tsp cumin seeds
- 1½ tbsp coriander seeds
- 1 cup / 200 g basmati rice
- 2 tbsp olive oil
- ½ tsp ground turmeric
- 1½ tsp ground allspice
- 1½ tsp ground cinnamon
- 1 tsp sugar
- 1½ cups / 350 ml water
- salt and freshly ground black pepper

INSTRUCTIONS
a) Place the lentils in a small saucepan, cover with plenty of water, bring to a boil, and cook for 12 to 15 minutes, until the lentils have softened but still have a little bite. Drain and set aside.

b) Peel the onions and slice thinly. Place on a large flat plate, sprinkle with the flour and 1 teaspoon salt, and mix well with your hands. Heat the sunflower oil in a medium heavy-bottomed saucepan placed over high heat. Make sure the oil is hot by throwing in a small piece of onion; it should sizzle vigorously. Reduce the heat to medium-high and carefully (it may spit!) add one-third of the sliced onion. Fry for 5 to 7 minutes, stirring occasionally with a slotted spoon, until the onion takes on a nice golden brown color and turns crispy (adjust the temperature so the onion doesn't fry too quickly and burn). Use the spoon to transfer the onion to a colander lined with paper towels and sprinkle with a little more salt. Do the same with the other two batches of onion; add a little extra oil if needed.

c) Wipe the saucepan in which you fried the onion clean and put in the cumin and coriander seeds. Place over medium heat and toast the seeds for a minute or two. Add the rice, olive oil, turmeric, allspice, cinnamon, sugar, ½ teaspoon salt, and plenty of black pepper. Stir to coat the rice with the oil and then add the cooked lentils and the water. Bring to a boil, cover with a lid, and simmer over very low heat for 15 minutes.
d) Remove from the heat, lift off the lid, and quickly cover the pan with a clean tea towel. Seal tightly with the lid and set aside for 10 minutes.
e) Finally, add half the fried onion to the rice and lentils and stir gently with a fork. Pile the mixture in a shallow serving bowl and top with the rest of the onion.

55. Hannukah Maqluba

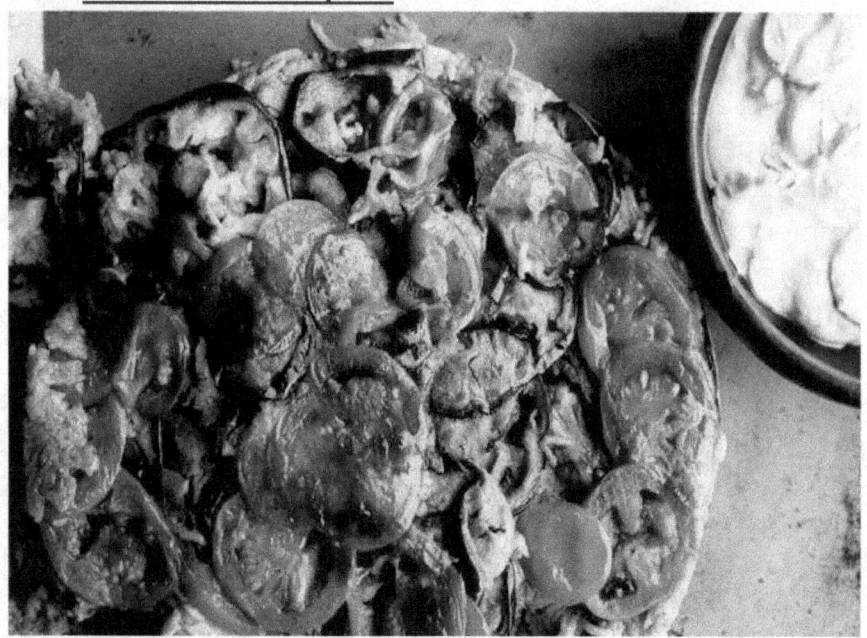

Makes: 4 TO 6

INGREDIENTS
- 2 medium eggplants (1½ lb / 650 g in total), cut into ¼-inch / 0.5cm slices
- 1⅔ cups / 320 g basmati rice
- 6 to 8 boneless chicken thighs, with the skin on, about 1¾ lb / 800 g in total
- 1 large onion, quartered lengthwise
- 10 black peppercorns
- 2 bay leaves
- 4 cups / 900 ml water
- sunflower oil, for frying
- 1 medium cauliflower (1 lb / 500 g), divided into large florets
- melted butter, for greasing the pan
- 3 to 4 medium ripe tomatoes (12 oz / 350 g in total), cut into ¼-inch / 0.5cm thick slices
- 4 large cloves garlic, halved
- 1 tsp ground turmeric
- 1 tsp ground cinnamon
- 1 tsp ground allspice
- ¼ tsp freshly ground black pepper
- 1 tsp baharat spice mix (store-bought or see recipe)
- 3½ tbsp / 30 g pine nuts, fried in 1 tbsp / 15 g ghee or unsalted butter until golden
- Yogurt with cucumber, to serve
- salt

INSTRUCTIONS

a) Place the eggplant slices on paper towels, sprinkle on both sides with salt, and leave for 20 minutes to lose some of the water.
b) Wash the rice and soak in plenty of cold water and 1 teaspoon salt for at least 30 minutes.
c) Meanwhile, heat a large saucepan over medium-high heat and sear the chicken for 3 to 4 minutes on each side, until golden brown (the chicken skin should produce enough oil to cook it; if needed, add a little sunflower oil). Add the onion, peppercorns, bay leaves, and water. Bring to a boil, then cover and cook over low heat for 20 minutes. Remove the chicken from the pan and set it aside. Strain the stock and reserve for later, skimming the fat.
d) While the chicken is cooking, heat a saucepan or Dutch oven, preferably nonstick and roughly 9½ inches / 24 cm in diameter and 5 inches / 12 cm deep, over medium-high heat. Add enough sunflower oil to come about ¾ inch / 2 cm up the sides of the pan. When you start seeing little bubbles surfacing, carefully (it may spit!) place some of the cauliflower florets in the oil and fry until golden brown, up to 3 minutes. Use a slotted spoon to transfer the first batch to paper towels and sprinkle with salt. Repeat with the remaining cauliflower.
e) Pat the eggplant slices dry with paper towels and fry them similarly in batches.
f) Remove the oil from the pan and wipe the pan clean. If it isn't a nonstick pan, line the bottom with a circle of parchment paper cut to the exact size and brush the sides with some melted butter. Now you are ready to layer the maqluba.
g) Start by arranging the slices of tomato in one layer, overlapping, followed by the eggplant slices. Next, arrange the cauliflower pieces and chicken thighs. Drain the rice well and spread it over the final layer and scatter the garlic pieces on top. Measure out a 3 cups / 700 ml of the reserved chicken stock and mix in all the spices, plus 1 teaspoon salt. Pour this over the rice and then

gently press it down with your hands, making sure all the rice is covered with stock. Add a little extra stock or water if needed.

h) Put the pan over medium heat and bring to a simmer; the stock doesn't need to simmer vigorously but you do need to make sure that it boils properly before covering the pan with a lid, decreasing the heat to low, and cooking over low heat for 30 minutes. Don't be tempted to uncover the pan; you'll need to allow the rice to steam properly. Remove the pan from the heat, take off the lid, and quickly place a clean tea towel over the pan, then seal with the lid again. Leave to rest for 10 minutes.

i) Once ready, remove the lid, invert a large round serving plate or platter over the open pan, and carefully but quickly invert the pan and plate together, holding both sides firmly. Leave the pan on the plate for 2 to 3 minutes, then slowly and carefully lift it off. Garnish with the pine nuts and serve with the Yogurt with cucumber.

56. Couscous with tomato and onion

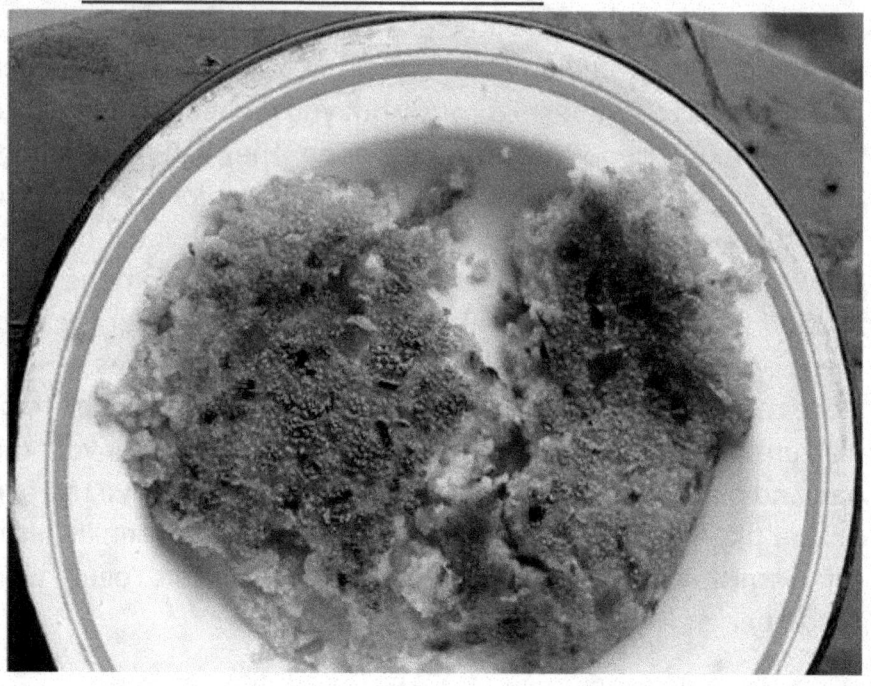

Makes: 4

INGREDIENTS
- 3 tbsp olive oil
- 1 medium onion, finely chopped (1 cup / 160 g in total)
- 1 tbsp tomato paste
- ½ tsp sugar
- 2 very ripe tomatoes, cut into ¼-inch / 0.5cm dice (1¾ cups / 320 g in total)
- 1 cup / 150 g couscous
- 1 cup / 220 ml boiling chicken or vegetable stock
- 2½ tbsp / 40 g unsalted butter
- salt and freshly ground black pepper

INSTRUCTIONS

a) Pour 2 tablespoons of the olive oil into a nonstick pan about 8½ inches / 22 cm in diameter and place over medium heat. Add the onion and cook for 5 minutes, stirring often, until it has softened but not colored. Stir in the tomato paste and sugar and cook for 1 minute. Add the tomatoes, ½ teaspoon salt, and some black pepper and cook for 3 minutes.

b) Meanwhile, put the couscous in a shallow bowl, pour over the boiling stock, and cover with plastic wrap. Set aside for 10 minutes, then remove the cover and fluff the couscous with a fork. Add the tomato sauce and stir well.

c) Wipe the pan clean and heat the butter and the remaining 1 tablespoon olive oil over medium heat. When the butter has melted, spoon the couscous into the pan and use the back of the spoon to pat it down gently so it is all packed in snugly. Cover the pan, reduce the heat to its lowest setting, and allow the couscous to steam for 10 to 12 minutes, until you can see a light brown color around the edges. Use an offset spatula or a knife to help you peer between the edge of the couscous and the side of the pan: you want a really crisp edge all over the base and sides.

d) Invert a large plate on top of the pan and quickly invert the pan and plate together, releasing the couscous onto the plate. Serve warm or at room temperature.

57. Watercress & chickpea soup with rose water

Makes: 4

INGREDIENTS
- 2 medium carrots (9 oz / 250 g in total), cut into ¾-inch / 2cm dice
- 3 tbsp olive oil
- 2½ tsp ras el hanout
- ½ tsp ground cinnamon
- 1½ cups / 240 g cooked chickpeas, fresh or canned
- 1 medium onion, thinly sliced
- 2½ tbsp / 15 g peeled and finely chopped fresh ginger
- 2½ cups / 600 ml vegetable stock
- 7 oz / 200 g watercress
- 3½ oz / 100 g spinach leaves
- 2 tsp superfine sugar
- 1 tsp rose water
- salt
- Greek yogurt, to serve (optional)
- Preheat the oven to 425°F / 220°C.

INSTRUCTIONS

a) Mix the carrots with 1 tablespoon of the olive oil, the ras el hanout, cinnamon, and a generous pinch of salt and spread flat in a roasting pan lined with parchment paper. Place in the oven for 15 minutes, then add half the chickpeas, stir well, and cook for another 10 minutes, until the carrot softens but still has a bite.

b) Meanwhile, place the onion and ginger in a large saucepan. Sauté with the remaining olive oil for about 10 minutes over medium heat, until the onion is completely soft and golden. Add the remaining chickpeas, stock, watercress, spinach, sugar, and ¾ teaspoon salt, stir well, and bring to a boil. Cook for a minute or two, just until the leaves wilt.

c) Using a food processor or blender, blitz the soup until smooth. Add the rose water, stir, taste, and add more salt or rose water if you like. Set aside until the carrot and chickpeas are ready, then reheat to serve.

d) To serve, divide the soup among four bowls and top with the hot carrot and chickpeas and, if you like, about 2 teaspoons yogurt per portion.

58. Hot yogurt & barley soup

Makes: 4

INGREDIENTS
- 6¾ cups / 1.6 liters water
- 1 cup / 200 g pearl barley
- 2 medium onions, finely chopped
- 1½ tsp dried mint
- 4 tbsp / 60 g unsalted butter
- 2 large eggs, beaten
- 2 cups / 400 g Greek yogurt
- ⅔ oz / 20 g fresh mint, chopped
- ⅓ oz / 10 g flat-leaf parsley, chopped
- 3 green onions, thinly sliced
- salt and freshly ground black pepper

INSTRUCTIONS
a) Bring the water to a boil with the barley in a large saucepan, adding 1 teaspoon salt, and simmer until the barley is cooked but still al dente, 15 to 20 minutes. Remove from the heat. Once cooked, you will need 4¾ cups / 1.1 liters of the cooking liquid for the soup; top up with water if you are left with less due to evaporation.

b) While the barley is cooking, sauté the onion and dried mint over medium heat in the butter until soft, about 15 minutes. Add this to the cooked barley.

c) Whisk together the eggs and yogurt in a large heatproof mixing bowl. Slowly mix in some of the barley and water, one ladle at a time, until the yogurt has warmed. This will temper the yogurt and eggs and stop them from splitting when added to the hot liquid. Add the yogurt to the soup pot and return to medium heat, stirring continuously, until the soup comes to a very light simmer. Remove from the heat, add the chopped herbs and green onions and check the seasoning. Serve hot.

59. Cannellini bean & lamb soup

Makes: 4

INGREDIENTS
- 1 tbsp sunflower oil
- 1 small onion (5 oz / 150 g in total), finely chopped
- ¼ small celery root, peeled and cut into ¼-inch / 0.5cm dice (6 oz / 170 g in total)
- 20 large cloves garlic, peeled but whole
- 1 tsp ground cumin
- 1 lb / 500 g lamb stew meat (or beef if you prefer), cut into ¾-inch / 2cm cubes
- 7 cups / 1.75 liters water
- ½ cup / 100 g dried cannellini or pinto beans, soaked overnight in plenty of cold water, then drained
- 7 cardamom pods, lightly crushed
- ½ tsp ground turmeric
- 2 tbsp tomato paste
- 1 tsp superfine sugar
- 9 oz / 250 g Yukon Gold or other yellow-fleshed potato, peeled and cut into ¾-inch / 2cm cubes
- salt and freshly ground black pepper
- bread, to serve
- freshly squeezed lemon juice, to serve
- chopped cilantro or Zhoug

INSTRUCTIONS
a) Heat the oil in a large frying pan and cook the onion and celery root over medium-high heat for 5 minutes, or until the onion starts to brown. Add the garlic cloves and cumin and cook for a further 2 minutes. Take off the heat and set aside.

b) Place the meat and water in a large saucepan or Dutch oven over medium-high heat, bring to a boil, lower the heat, and simmer for 10 minutes, skimming the surface frequently until you get a clear broth. Add the onion and celery root mix, the drained beans, cardamom, turmeric, tomato paste, and sugar. Bring to a boil, cover, and simmer gently for 1 hour, or until the meat is tender.

c) Add the potatoes to the soup and season with 1 teaspoon salt and ½ teaspoon black pepper. Bring back to a boil, lower the heat, and simmer, uncovered, for a further 20 minutes, or until the potatoes and beans are tender. The soup should be thick. Let it bubble away a bit longer, if needed, to reduce, or add some water. Taste and add more seasoning to your liking. Serve the soup with bread and some lemon juice and fresh chopped cilantro, or zhoug.

60. Seafood & Fennel Soup

Makes: 4

INGREDIENTS
- 2 tbsp olive oil
- 4 cloves garlic, thinly sliced
- 2 fennel bulbs (10½ oz / 300 g in total), trimmed and cut into thin wedges
- 1 large waxy potato (7 oz / 200 g in total), peeled and cut into ⅔-inch / 1.5cm cubes
- 3 cups / 700 ml fish stock (or chicken or vegetable stock, if preferred)
- ½ medium preserved lemon (½ oz / 15 g in total), store-bought or see recipe
- 1 red chile, sliced (optional)
- 6 tomatoes (14 oz / 400 g in total), peeled and cut into quarters
- 1 tbsp sweet paprika
- good pinch of saffron
- 4 tbsp finely chopped flat-leaf parsley
- 4 fillets sea bass (about 10½ oz / 300 g in total), skin on, cut in half
- 14 mussels (about 8 oz / 220 g in total)
- 15 clams (about 4½ oz / 140 g in total)
- 10 tiger prawns (about 8 oz / 220 g in total), in their shells or peeled and deveined
- 3 tbsp arak, ouzo, or Pernod
- 2 tsp chopped tarragon (optional)
- salt and freshly ground black pepper

INSTRUCTIONS

a) Place the olive oil and garlic in a wide, low-rimmed frying pan and cook over medium heat for 2 minutes without coloring the garlic. Stir in the fennel and potato and cook for a further 3 to 4 minutes. Add the stock and preserved lemon, season with ¼ teaspoon salt and some black pepper, bring to a boil, then cover and cook over low heat for 12 to 14 minutes, until the potatoes are cooked. Add the chile (if using), tomatoes, spices, and half the parsley and cook for a further 4 to 5 minutes.

b) Add up to another 1¼ cups / 300 ml of water at this point, simply as much as is needed to be able just to cover the fish to poach it, and bring to a simmer again. Add the sea bass and shellfish, cover the pan, and allow to boil quite fiercely for 3 to 4 minutes, until the shellfish open and the prawns turn pink.

c) Using a slotted spoon, remove the fish and shellfish from the soup. If it is still a bit watery, allow the soup to boil for a few more minutes to reduce. Add the arak and taste for seasoning.

d) Finally, return the shellfish and fish to the soup to reheat them. Serve at once, garnished with the remainder of the parsley and the tarragon, if using.

61. Pistachio soup

Makes: 4

INGREDIENTS
- 2 tbsp boiling water
- ¼ tsp saffron threads
- 1⅔ cups / 200 g shelled unsalted pistachios
- 2 tbsp / 30 g unsalted butter
- 4 shallots, finely chopped (3½ oz / 100 g in total)
- 1 oz / 25 g ginger, peeled and finely chopped
- 1 leek, finely chopped (1¼ cups / 150 g in total)
- 2 tsp ground cumin
- 3 cups / 700 ml chicken stock
- ⅓ cup / 80 ml freshly squeezed orange juice
- 1 tbsp freshly squeezed lemon juice
- salt and freshly ground black pepper
- sour cream, to serve

INSTRUCTIONS
a) Preheat the oven to 350°F / 180°C. Pour the boiling water over the saffron threads in a small cup and leave to infuse for 30 minutes.

b) To remove the pistachio skins, blanch the nuts in boiling water for 1 minute, drain, and while still hot, remove the skins by pressing the nuts between your fingers. Not all the skins will come off as with almonds—this is fine as it won't affect the soup—but getting rid of some skin will improve the color, making it a brighter green. Spread the pistachios out on a baking sheet and roast in the oven for 8 minutes. Remove and leave to cool.

c) Heat the butter in a large saucepan and add the shallots, ginger, leek, cumin, ½ teaspoon salt, and some black pepper. Sauté over medium heat for 10 minutes, stirring often, until the shallots are completely soft. Add the stock and half of the saffron liquid. Cover the pan, lower the heat, and let the soup simmer for 20 minutes.

d) Place all but 1 tablespoon of the pistachios in a large bowl along with half of the soup. Use a handheld blender to blitz until smooth and then return this to the saucepan. Add the orange and lemon juice, reheat, and taste to adjust the seasoning.
e) To serve, coarsely chop up the reserved pistachios. Transfer the hot soup into bowls and top with a spoonful of sour cream. Sprinkle with the pistachios and drizzle with the remaining saffron liquid.

62. Burnt Eggplant & Mograbieh Soup

Makes: 4

INGREDIENTS
- 5 small eggplants (about 2½ lb / 1.2 kg in total)
- sunflower oil, for frying
- 1 onion, sliced (about 1 cup / 125 g in total)
- 1 tbsp cumin seeds, freshly ground
- 1½ tsp tomato paste
- 2 large tomatoes (12 oz / 350 g in total), skinned and diced
- 1½ cups / 350 ml chicken or vegetable stock
- 1⅔ cups / 400 ml water
- 4 cloves garlic, crushed
- 2½ tsp sugar
- 2 tbsp freshly squeezed lemon juice
- ⅓ cup / 100 g mograbieh, or alternative, such as maftoul, fregola, or giant couscous (see section on Couscous)
- 2 tbsp shredded basil, or 1 tbsp chopped dill, optional
- salt and freshly ground black pepper

INSTRUCTIONS
a) Start by burning three of the eggplants. To do this, follow the instructions for Burnt eggplant with garlic, lemon, and pomegranate seeds.
b) Cut the remaining eggplants into ⅔-inch / 1.5cm dice. Heat about ⅔ cup / 150 ml oil in a large saucepan over medium-high heat. When it is hot, add the eggplant dice. Fry for 10 to 15 minutes, stirring often, until colored all over; add a little more oil if needed so there is always some oil in the pan. Remove the eggplant, place in a colander to drain, and sprinkle with salt.
c) Make sure you have about 1 tablespoon oil left in the pan, then add the onion and cumin and sauté for about 7 minutes, stirring often. Add the tomato paste and cook for another minute before adding the tomatoes, stock, water, garlic, sugar, lemon juice, 1½ teaspoons salt, and some black pepper. Simmer gently for 15 minutes.

d) Meanwhile, bring a small saucepan of salted water to a boil and add the mograbieh or alternative. Cook until al dente; this will vary according to brand but should take 15 to 18 minutes (check the packet). Drain and refresh under cold water.
e) Transfer the burnt eggplant flesh to the soup and blitz to a smooth liquid with a handheld blender. Add the mograbieh and fried eggplant, keeping some to garnish at the end, and simmer for another 2 minutes. Taste and adjust the seasoning. Serve hot, with the reserved mograbieh and fried eggplant on top and garnished with basil or dill, if you like.

63. Tomato & sourdough soup

Makes: 4

INGREDIENTS
- 2 tbsp olive oil, plus extra to finish
- 1 large onion, chopped (1⅔ cups / 250 g in total)
- 1 tsp cumin seeds
- 2 cloves garlic, crushed
- 3 cups / 750 ml vegetable stock
- 4 large ripe tomatoes, chopped (4 cups / 650 g in total)
- one 14-oz / 400g can chopped Italian tomatoes
- 1 tbsp superfine sugar
- 1 slice sourdough bread (1½ oz / 40 g in total)
- 2 tbsp chopped cilantro, plus extra to finish
- salt and freshly ground black pepper

INSTRUCTIONS
a) Heat the oil in a medium saucepan and add the onion. Sauté for about 5 minutes, stirring often, until the onion is translucent. Add the cumin and garlic and fry for 2 minutes. Pour in the stock, both types of tomato, sugar, 1 teaspoon salt, and a good grind of black pepper.

b) Bring the soup to a gentle simmer and cook for 20 minutes, adding the bread, torn into chunks, halfway through the cooking. Finally, add the cilantro and then blitz, using a blender, in a few pulses so that the tomatoes break down but are still a little coarse and chunky. The soup should be quite thick; add a little water if it is too thick at this point. Serve, drizzled with oil and scattered with fresh cilantro.

64. Clear chicken soup with knaidlach

Makes: 4

INGREDIENTS
- 1 free-range chicken, about 4½ lb / 2 kg, divided into quarters, with all the bones, plus giblets if you can get them and any extra wings or bones you can get from the butcher
- 1½ tsp sunflower oil
- 1 cup / 250 ml dry white wine
- 2 carrots, peeled and cut into ¾-inch / 2cm slices (2 cups / 250 g in total)
- 4 celery stalks (about 10½ oz / 300 g in total), cut into 2½-inch / 6cm segments
- 2 medium onions (about 12 oz / 350 g in total), cut into 8 wedges
- 1 large turnip (7 oz / 200 g), peeled, trimmed, and cut into 8 segments
- 2 oz / 50 g bunch flat-leaf parsley
- 2 oz / 50 g bunch cilantro
- 5 thyme sprigs
- 1 small rosemary sprig
- ¾ oz / 20 g dill, plus extra to garnish
- 3 bay leaves
- 3½ oz / 100 g fresh ginger, thinly sliced
- 20 black peppercorns
- 5 allspice berries
- salt

KNAIDLACH (Makes: 12 TO 15)
- 2 extra-large eggs
- 2½ tbsp / 40 g margarine or chicken fat, melted and allowed to cool a bit
- 2 tbsp finely chopped flat-leaf parsley
- ⅔ cup / 75 g matzo meal
- 4 tbsp soda water
- salt and freshly ground black pepper

INSTRUCTIONS

a) To make the knaidlach, whisk the eggs in a medium bowl until frothy. Whisk in the melted margarine, then ½ teaspoon salt, some black pepper, and the parsley. Gradually, stir in the matzo meal, followed by the soda water, and stir to a uniform paste. Cover the bowl and chill the batter until cold and firm, at least an hour or two and up to 1 day ahead.

b) Line a baking sheet with plastic wrap. Using your wet hands and a spoon, shape the batter into balls the size of small walnuts and place on the baking sheet.

c) Drop the matzo balls into a large pot of gently boiling salted water. Cover partially with a lid and decrease the heat to low. Simmer gently until tender, about 30 minutes.

d) Using a slotted spoon, transfer the knaidlach onto a clean baking sheet where they can cool down, and then be chilled for up to a day. Or, they can go straight into the hot soup.

e) For the soup, trim any excess fat off the chicken and discard. Pour the oil into a very large saucepan or Dutch oven and sear the chicken pieces over high heat on all sides, 3 to 4 minutes. Remove from the pan, discard the oil, and wipe the pan. Add the wine and let it bubble away for a minute. Return the chicken, cover with water, and bring to a very gentle simmer. Simmer for about 10 minutes, skimming away the scum. Add the carrots, celery, onions, and turnip. Tie all the herbs into a bundle with string and add to the pot. Add the bay leaves, ginger, peppercorns, allspice, and 1½ teaspoons salt and then pour in enough water to cover everything well.

f) Bring the soup back to a very gentle simmer and cook for 1½ hours, skimming occasionally and adding water as needed to keep everything well covered. Lift the chicken from the soup and remove the meat from the bones. Keep the meat in a bowl with a little broth to keep it moist, and refrigerate; reserve for another use. Return the bones to the pot and simmer for another hour, adding just enough water to keep the bones and vegetables covered. Strain the hot soup and discard the herbs, vegetables, and bones. Warm the cooked knaidlach in the soup. Once they are hot, serve the soup and knaidlach in shallow bowls, sprinkled with dill.

65. Spicy freekeh soup with meatballs

Makes: 6
MEATBALLS

INGREDIENTS
- 14 oz / 400 g ground beef, lamb, or a combination of both
- 1 small onion (5 oz / 150 g in total), finely diced
- 2 tbsp finely chopped flat-leaf parsley
- ½ tsp ground allspice
- ¼ tsp ground cinnamon
- 3 tbsp all-purpose flour
- 2 tbsp olive oil
- salt and freshly ground black pepper
- SOUP
- 2 tbsp olive oil
- 1 large onion (9 oz / 250 g in total), chopped
- 3 cloves garlic, crushed
- 2 carrots (9 oz / 250 g in total), peeled and cut into ⅜-inch / 1cm cubes
- 2 celery stalks (5 oz / 150 g in total), cut into ⅜-inch / 1cm cubes
- 3 large tomatoes (12 oz / 350 g in total), chopped
- 2½ tbsp / 40 g tomato paste
- 1 tbsp baharat spice mix (store-bought or see recipe)
- 1 tbsp ground coriander
- 1 cinnamon stick
- 1 tbsp superfine sugar
- 1 cup / 150 g cracked freekeh
- 2 cups / 500 ml beef stock
- 2 cups / 500 ml chicken stock
- 3¼ cups / 800 ml hot water
- ⅓ oz / 10 g cilantro, chopped
- 1 lemon, cut into 6 wedges

INSTRUCTIONS

a) Start with the meatballs. In a large bowl, mix together the meat, onion, parsley, allspice, cinnamon, ½ teaspoon salt, and ¼ teaspoon pepper. Using your hands, mix well, then form the mixture into Ping-Pong-size balls and roll them in the flour; you will get about 15. Heat the olive oil in a large Dutch oven and fry the meatballs over medium heat for a few minutes, until golden brown on all sides. Remove the meatballs and set aside.

b) Wipe out the pan with paper towels and add the olive oil for the soup. Over medium heat, fry the onion and garlic for 5 minutes. Stir in the carrots and celery and cook for 2 minutes. Add the tomatoes, tomato paste, spices, sugar, 2 teaspoons salt, and ½ teaspoon pepper and cook for 1 more minute. Stir in the freekeh and cook for 2 to 3 minutes. Add the stocks, hot water, and meatballs. Bring to a boil, lower the heat, and simmer very gently for a further 35 to 45 minutes, stirring occasionally, until the freekeh is plump and tender. The soup should be quite thick. Reduce or add a little water as needed. Finally, taste and adjust the seasoning.

c) Ladle the hot soup into serving bowls and sprinkle with the cilantro. Serve the lemon wedges on the side.

66. Lamb-Stuffed Quince with Pomegranate & Cilantro

Makes: 4

INGREDIENTS
- 14 oz / 400 g ground lamb
- 1 clove garlic, crushed
- 1 red chile, chopped
- ⅔ oz / 20 g cilantro, chopped, plus 2 tbsp, to garnish
- ½ cup / 50 g bread crumbs
- 1 tsp ground allspice
- 2 tbsp finely grated fresh ginger
- 2 medium onions, finely chopped (1⅓ cups / 220 g in total)
- 1 large free-range egg
- 4 quince (2¾ lb / 1.3 kg in total)
- juice of ½ lemon, plus 1 tbsp freshly squeezed lemon juice
- 3 tbsp olive oil
- 8 cardamom pods
- 2 tsp pomegranate molasses
- 2 tsp sugar
- 2 cups / 500 ml chicken stock
- seeds of ½ pomegranate
- salt and freshly ground black pepper

INSTRUCTIONS

a) Place the lamb in a mixing bowl along with the garlic, chile, cilantro, bread crumbs, allspice, half of the ginger, half of the onion, egg, ¾ teaspoon salt, and some pepper. Mix well with your hands and set aside.

b) Peel the quince and halve them lengthwise. Put them in a bowl of cold water with the juice of the ½ lemon so that they do not turn brown. Use a melon baller or small spoon to remove the seeds and then hollow out the quince halves so that you are left with a ⅔-inch / 1.5cm shell. Keep the scooped-out flesh. Fill the hollows with the lamb mix, using your hands to push it down.

c) Heat the olive oil in a large frying pan for which you have a lid. Place the reserved quince flesh in a food processor, blitz to chop well, and then transfer the mixture to the pan along with the remaining onion, ginger, and the cardamom pods. Sauté for 10 to 12 minutes, until the onion has softened. Add the molasses, the 1 tablespoon lemon juice, sugar, stock, ½ teaspoon salt, and some black pepper and mix well. Add the quince halves to the sauce, with the meat stuffing facing upward, lower the heat to a gentle simmer, cover the pan, and cook for about 30 minutes. At the end the quince should be completely soft, the meat well cooked, and the sauce thick. Lift the lid and simmer for a minute or two to reduce the sauce if needed.

d) Serve warm or at room temperature, sprinkled with the cilantro and pomegranate seeds.

67. Turnip & veal "cake"

Makes: 4

INGREDIENTS
- 1⅔ cups / 300 g basmati rice
- 14 oz / 400 g ground veal, lamb, or beef
- ½ cup / 30 g chopped flat-leaf parsley
- 1½ tsp baharat spice mix (store-bought or see recipe)
- ½ tsp ground cinnamon
- ½ tsp chile flakes
- 2 tbsp olive oil
- 10 to 15 medium turnips (3¼ lb / 1.5 kg in total)
- about 1⅔ cups / 400 ml sunflower oil
- 2 cups / 300 g chopped tomatoes, canned are fine
- 1½ tbsp tamarind paste
- ¾ cup plus 2 tbsp / 200 ml chicken stock, hot
- 1 cup / 250 ml water
- 1½ tbsp superfine sugar
- 2 thyme sprigs, leaves picked
- salt and freshly ground black pepper

INSTRUCTIONS

a) Wash the rice and drain well. Place in a large mixing bowl and add the meat, parsley, baharat, cinnamon, 2 teaspoons salt, ½ teaspoon pepper, chile, and olive oil. Mix well and set aside.

b) Peel the turnips and cut them into slices ⅜ inch / 1 cm thick. Heat enough sunflower oil over medium-high heat to come ¾ inch / 2 cm up the sides of a large frying pan. Fry the turnip slices in batches for 3 to 4 minutes per batch, until golden. Transfer to a plate lined with paper towels, sprinkle with a little salt, and allow to cool down.

c) Put the tomatoes, tamarind, stock, water, sugar, 1 teaspoon salt, and ½ teaspoon pepper in a large mixing bowl. Whisk well. Pour about one-third of this liquid into a medium, heavy-bottomed saucepan (9½ inches / 24 cm in diameter). Arrange one-third of the turnip slices inside. Add half the rice mixture and level.

Arrange another layer of turnips, followed by the second half of the rice. Finish with the last of the turnips, pressing down softly with your hands. Pour the remaining tomato liquid over the turnip and rice layers and sprinkle with the thyme. Gently slide a spatula down the sides of the pot to allow the juices to flow to the bottom.

d) Place over medium heat and bring to a boil. Lower the heat to an absolute minimum, cover, and simmer for 1 hour. Take off the heat, uncover, and allow to rest for 10 to 15 minutes before serving. Unfortunately, it is impossible to invert the cake onto a plate as it doesn't hold its shape, so it must be spooned out.

68. Hannukah Stuffed onions

Makes: ABOUT 16 STUFFED ONIONS

INGREDIENTS
- 4 large onions (2 lb / 900 g in total, peeled weight) about 1⅔ cups / 400 ml vegetable stock
- 1½ tbsp pomegranate molasses
- salt and freshly ground black pepper
- STUFFING
- 1½ tbsp olive oil
- 1 cup / 150 g finely chopped shallots
- ½ cup / 100 g short-grain rice
- ¼ cup / 35 g pine nuts, crushed
- 2 tbsp chopped fresh mint
- 2 tbsp chopped flat-leaf parsley
- 2 tsp dried mint
- 1 tsp ground cumin
- ⅛ tsp ground clove
- ¼ tsp ground allspice
- ¾ tsp salt
- ½ tsp freshly ground black pepper
- 4 lemon wedges (optional)

INSTRUCTIONS

a) Peel and cut about ¼ inch / 0.5 cm off the tops and tails of the onions, place the trimmed onions in a large saucepan with plenty of water, bring to a boil, and cook for 15 minutes. Drain and set aside to cool down.

b) To prepare the stuffing, heat the olive oil in a medium frying pan over medium-high heat and add the shallots. Sauté for 8 minutes, stirring often, then add all the remaining ingredients except the lemon wedges. Turn the heat to low and continue to cook and stir for 10 minutes.

c) Using a small knife, make a long cut from the top of the onion to the bottom, running all the way to its center, so that each layer of onion has only one slit running through it. Start gently separating the onion layers, one after another, until you reach the core. Don't worry if some of the layers tear a little through the peeling; you can still use them.

d) Hold a layer of onion in one cupped hand and spoon about 1 tablespoon of the rice mixture into one-half of the onion, placing the filling near to one end of the opening. Don't be tempted to fill it up more, as it needs to be wrapped up nice and snug. Fold the empty side of the onion over the stuffed side and roll it up tightly so the rice is covered with a few layers of onion with no air in the middle. Place in a medium frying pan for which you have a lid, seam side down, and continue with the remaining onions and rice mixture. Lay the onions side by side in the pan, so that there is no space to move about. Fill any spaces with parts of the onion that have not been stuffed. Add enough stock so that the onions are three-quarters covered, along with the pomegranate molasses, and season with ¼ teaspoon salt.

e) Cover the pan and cook on the lowest possible simmer for 1½ to 2 hours, until the liquid has evaporated. Serve warm or at room temperature, with lemon wedges if you like.

69. Hannukah Open Kibbeh

Makes: 6

INGREDIENTS
- 1 cup / 125 g fine bulgur wheat
- 1 cup / 200 ml water
- 6 tbsp / 90 ml olive oil
- 2 cloves garlic, crushed
- 2 medium onions, finely chopped
- 1 green chile, finely chopped
- 12 oz / 350 g ground lamb
- 1 tsp ground allspice
- 1 tsp ground cinnamon
- 1 tsp ground coriander
- 2 tbsp coarsely chopped cilantro
- ½ cup / 60 g pine nuts
- 3 tbsp coarsely chopped flat-leaf parsley
- 2 tbsp self-rising flour, plus a little extra if needed
- 3½ tbsp / 50 g light tahini paste
- 2 tsp freshly squeezed lemon juice
- 1 tsp sumac
- salt and freshly ground black pepper

INSTRUCTIONS
a) Preheat the oven to 400°F / 200°C. Line an 8-inch / 20cm springform pan with waxed paper.
b) Place the bulgur in a large bowl and cover it with the water. Leave for 30 minutes.
c) Meanwhile, heat 4 tablespoons of the olive oil in a large frying pan over medium-high heat. Sauté the garlic, onion, and chile until they are completely soft. Remove everything from the pan, return it to high heat, and add the lamb. Cook for 5 minutes, stirring continuously, until brown.
d) Return the onion mixture to the pan and add the spices, cilantro, ½ teaspoon salt, a generous grind of black pepper, and most of the pine nuts and parsley, leaving some aside. Cook for a couple

of minutes, remove from the heat, taste, and adjust the seasoning.

e) Check the bulgur to see if all the water has been absorbed. Drain to remove any remaining liquid. Add the flour, 1 tablespoon of the olive oil, ¼ teaspoon salt, and a pinch of black pepper and use your hands to work everything into a pliable mixture that just holds together; add a little bit more flour if the mixture is very sticky. Push firmly onto the bottom of the springform pan so that it is compacted and leveled. Spread the lamb mixture evenly on top and press it down a little. Bake for about 20 minutes, until the meat is quite dark brown and very hot.

f) While you wait, whisk together the tahini paste with the lemon juice, 3½ tbsp / 50 ml water, and a pinch of salt. You are after a very thick, yet pourable sauce. If needed, add a little extra water.

g) Remove the kibbeh cake from the oven, spread the tahini sauce evenly on top, sprinkle with the reserved pine nuts and chopped parsley, and return to the oven immediately. Bake for 10 to 12 minutes, until the tahini is just setting and has taken on a little bit of color, and the pine nuts are golden.

h) Remove from the oven and let cool until warm or at room temperature. Before serving, sprinkle the top with the sumac and drizzle with the remaining oil. Carefully remove the pan sides and cut the kibbeh into slices. Lift them gently so they don't break.

70. Kubbeh hamusta

Makes: 6

INGREDIENTS

KUBBEH STUFFING
- 1½ tbsp sunflower oil
- ½ medium onion, very finely chopped (½ cup / 75 g in total)
- 12 oz / 350 g ground beef
- ½ tsp ground allspice
- 1 large clove garlic, crushed
- 2 pale celery stalks, very finely chopped, or an equal amount of chopped celery leaves (½ cup / 60 g in total)
- salt and freshly ground black pepper
- KUBBEH CASES
- 2 cups / 325 g semolina
- 5 tbsp / 40 g all-purpose flour
- 1 cup / 220 ml hot water
- SOUP
- 4 cloves garlic, crushed
- 5 celery stalks, leaves picked and stalks cut on an angle into ⅔-inch / 1.5cm slices (2 cups / 230 g in total)
- 10½ oz / 300 g Swiss chard leaves, green part only, cut into ⅔-inch / 2cm strips
- 2 tbsp sunflower oil
- 1 large onion, coarsely chopped (1¼ cups / 200 g in total)
- 2 quarts / 2 liters chicken stock
- 1 large zucchini, cut into ⅜-inch / 1cm cubes (1⅔ cups / 200 g in total)
- 6½ tbsp / 100 ml freshly squeezed lemon juice, plus extra if needed
- lemon wedges, to serve

INSTRUCTIONS

a) First, prepare the meat stuffing. Heat the oil in a medium frying pan, and add the onion. Cook over medium heat until translucent, about 5 minutes. Add the beef, allspice, ¾ teaspoon salt, and a good grind of black pepper and stir as you cook for 3 minutes, just to brown. Reduce the heat to medium-low and allow the meat to cook slowly for about 20 minutes, until completely dry, stirring from time to time. At the end, add the garlic and celery, cook for another 3 minutes, and remove from the heat. Taste and adjust the seasoning. Allow to cool down.

b) While the beef mix is cooking, prepare the kubbeh cases. Mix the semolina, flour, and ¼ teaspoon salt in a large mixing bowl. Gradually add the water, stirring with a wooden spoon and then your hands until you get a sticky dough. Cover with a damp cloth and set aside to rest for 15 minutes.

c) Knead the dough for a few minutes on a work surface. It must be supple and spreadable without cracking. Add a little water or flour if needed. To make the dumplings, get a bowl of water and wet your hands (make sure your hands are wet throughout the process to prevent sticking). Take a piece of dough weighing about 1 oz / 30 g and flatten it in your palm; you're aiming for disks 4 inches / 10 cm in diameter. Place about 2 teaspoons of the stuffing in the center. Fold the edges over the stuffing to cover and then seal it inside. Roll the kubbeh between your hands to form a ball and then press it down into a round, flat shape about 1¼ inches / 3 cm thick. Place the dumplings on a tray covered with plastic wrap and drizzled with a little water and leave to one side.

d) For the soup, place the garlic, half the celery, and half the chard in a food processor and blitz to a coarse paste. Heat the oil in a large saucepan over medium heat and sauté the onion for about 10 minutes, until pale golden. Add the celery and chard paste and cook for 3 minutes more. Add the stock, zucchini, the remaining celery and chard, the lemon juice, 1 teaspoon salt, and ½ teaspoon black pepper. Bring to a boil and cook for 10 minutes, then taste and adjust the seasoning. It needs to be sharp, so add another tablespoon of lemon juice if you need to.

e) Finally, carefully add the kubbeh to the soup—a few at a time, so they don't stick to one another—and simmer gently for 20 minutes. Leave aside for a good half hour for them to settle and soften, then reheat and serve. Accompany with a wedge of lemon for an extra lemony kick.

71. Stuffed Romano Peppers

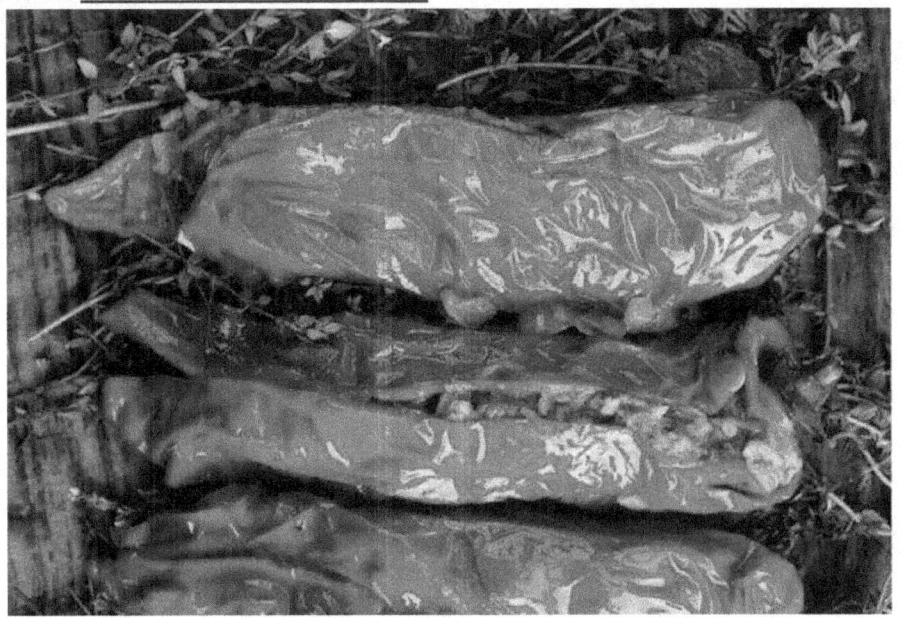

Makes: 4 GENEROUSLY

INGREDIENTS
- 8 medium Romano or other sweet peppers
- 1 large tomato, coarsely chopped (1 cup / 170 g in total)
- 2 medium onions, coarsely chopped (1⅔ cups / 250 g in total)
- about 2 cups / 500 ml vegetable stock
- STUFFING
- ¾ cup / 140 g basmati rice
- 1½ tbsp baharat spice mix (store-bought or see recipe)
- ½ tsp ground cardamom
- 2 tbsp olive oil
- 1 large onion, finely chopped (1⅓ cups / 200 g in total)
- 14 oz / 400 g ground lamb
- 2½ tbsp chopped flat-leaf parsley
- 2 tbsp chopped dill
- 1½ tbsp dried mint
- 1½ tsp sugar
- salt and freshly ground black pepper

INSTRUCTIONS

a) Start with the stuffing. Place the rice in a saucepan and cover with lightly salted water. Bring to a boil and then cook for 4 minutes. Drain, refresh under cold water, and set aside.

b) Dry-fry the spices in a frying pan. Add the olive oil and onion and fry for about 7 minutes, stirring often, until the onion is soft. Pour this, along with the rice, meat, herbs, sugar, and 1 teaspoon salt into a large mixing bowl. Use your hands to mix everything together well.

c) Starting from the stalk end, use a small knife to cut lengthwise three-quarters of the way down each pepper, without removing the stalk, creating a long opening. Without forcing the pepper open too much, remove the seeds and then stuff each pepper with an equal amount of the mixture.

d) Place the chopped tomato and onion in a very large frying pan for which you have a tight-fitting lid. Arrange the peppers on top, close together, and pour in just enough stock so that it comes inch / 1 cm up the sides of the peppers. Season with ½ teaspoon salt and some black pepper. Cover the pan with a lid and simmer over the lowest possible heat for an hour. It is important that the filling is just steamed, so the lid must fit tightly; make sure there is always a little bit of liquid at the bottom of the pan. Serve the peppers warm, not hot, or at room temperature.

72. Stuffed Eggplant with Lamb & Pine Nuts

Makes: 4 GENEROUSLY

INGREDIENTS
- 4 medium eggplants (about 2½ lb / 1.2 kg), halved lengthwise
- 6 tbsp / 90 ml olive oil
- 1½ tsp ground cumin
- 1½ tbsp sweet paprika
- 1 tbsp ground cinnamon
- 2 medium onions (12 oz / 340 g in total), finely chopped
- 1 lb / 500 g ground lamb
- 7 tbsp / 50 g pine nuts
- ⅔ oz / 20 g flat-leaf parsley, chopped
- 2 tsp tomato paste
- 3 tsp superfine sugar
- ⅔ cup / 150 ml water
- 1½ tbsp freshly squeezed lemon juice
- 1 tsp tamarind paste
- 4 cinnamon sticks
- salt and freshly ground black pepper

INSTRUCTIONS
a) Preheat the oven to 425°F / 220°C.
b) Place the eggplant halves, skin side down, in a roasting pan large enough to accommodate them snugly. Brush the flesh with 4 tablespoons of the olive oil and season with 1 teaspoon salt and plenty of black pepper. Roast for about 20 minutes, until golden brown. Remove from the oven and allow to cool slightly.
c) While the eggplants are cooking, you can start making the stuffing by heating the remaining 2 tablespoons olive oil in a large frying pan. Mix together the cumin, paprika, and ground cinnamon and add half of this spice mix to the pan, along with the onions. Cook over medium-high heat for about 8 minutes, stirring often, before adding the lamb, pine nuts, parsley, tomato paste, 1 teaspoon of the sugar, 1 teaspoon salt, and some black

pepper. Continue to cook and stir for another 8 minutes, until the meat is cooked.

d) Place the remaining spice mix in a bowl and add the water, lemon juice, tamarind, the remaining 2 teaspoons sugar, the cinnamon sticks, and ½ teaspoon salt; mix well.

e) Reduce the oven temperature to 375°F / 195°C. Pour the spice mix into the bottom of the eggplant roasting pan. Spoon the lamb mixture on top of each eggplant. Cover the pan tightly with aluminum foil, return to the oven, and roast for 1½ hours, by which point the eggplants should be completely soft and the sauce thick; twice during the cooking, remove the foil and baste the eggplants with the sauce, adding some water if the sauce dries out. Serve warm, not hot, or at room temperature.

73. Stuffed potatoes

Makes: 4 TO 6

INGREDIENTS
- 1 lb / 500 g ground beef
- about 2 cups / 200 g white bread crumbs
- 1 medium onion, finely chopped (¾ cup / 120 g in total)
- 2 cloves garlic, crushed
- ⅔ oz / 20 g flat-leaf parsley, finely chopped
- 2 tbsp thyme leaves, chopped
- 1½ tsp ground cinnamon
- 2 large free-range eggs, beaten
- 3¼ lb / 1.5 kg medium Yukon Gold potatoes, about 3¾ by 2¼ inches / 9 by 6 cm, peeled and halved lengthwise
- 2 tbsp chopped cilantro
- salt and freshly ground black pepper

TOMATO SAUCE
- 2 tbsp olive oil
- 5 cloves garlic, crushed
- 1 medium onion, finely chopped (¾ cup / 120 g in total)
- 1½ celery stalks, finely chopped (⅔ cup / 80 g in total)
- 1 small carrot, peeled and finely chopped (½ cup / 70 g in total)
- 1 red chile, finely chopped
- 1½ tsp ground cumin
- 1 tsp ground allspice
- pinch of smoked paprika
- 1½ tsp sweet paprika
- 1 tsp caraway seeds, crushed with a mortar and pestle or spice grinder
- one 28-oz / 800g can chopped tomatoes
- 1 tbsp tamarind paste
- 1½ tsp superfine sugar

INSTRUCTIONS

a) Start with the tomato sauce. Heat the olive oil in the widest frying pan you have; you will also need a lid for it. Add the garlic, onion, celery, carrot, and chile and sauté over low heat for 10 minutes, until the vegetables are soft. Add the spices, stir well, and cook for 2 to 3 minutes. Pour in the chopped tomatoes, tamarind, sugar, ½ teaspoon salt, and some black pepper and bring to a boil. Remove from the heat.

b) To make the stuffed potatoes, place the beef, bread crumbs, onion, garlic, parsley, thyme, cinnamon, 1 teaspoon salt, some black pepper, and the eggs in a mixing bowl. Use your hands to combine all the ingredients well.

c) Hollow out each potato half with a melon baller or a teaspoon, creating shell ⅔ inch / 1.5 cm thick. Stuff the meat mixture into each cavity, using your hands to push it right down so that it fills the potato completely. Carefully press all the potatoes down into the tomato sauce so that they are sitting close together, with the meat stuffing facing upward. Add about 1¼ cups / 300 ml water, or just enough to almost cover the patties with sauce, bring to a light simmer, cover the pan with a lid, and leave to cook slowly for at least 1 hour or even longer, until the sauce is thick and the potatoes are very soft. If the sauce hasn't thickened enough, remove the lid and reduce for 5 to 10 minutes. Serve hot or warm, garnished with the cilantro.

74. Stuffed artichokes with peas & dill

Makes: 4

INGREDIENTS
- 14 oz / 400 g leeks, trimmed and cut into ¼-inch / 0.5cm slices
- 9 oz / 250 g ground beef
- 1 large free-range egg
- 1 tsp ground allspice
- 1 tsp ground cinnamon
- 2 tsp dried mint
- 12 medium globe artichokes or thawed frozen artichoke bottoms (see introduction)
- 6 tbsp / 90 ml freshly squeezed lemon juice, plus juice of ½ lemon if using fresh artichokes
- ⅓ cup / 80 ml olive oil
- all-purpose flour, for coating the artichokes
- about 2 cups / 500 ml chicken or vegetable stock
- 1⅓ cups / 200 g frozen peas
- ⅓ oz / 10 g dill, coarsely chopped
- salt and freshly ground black pepper

INSTRUCTIONS

a) Blanch the leeks in boiling water for 5 minutes. Drain, refresh, and squeeze out the water.

b) Coarsely chop the leeks and place in a mixing bowl along with the meat, egg, spices, mint, 1 teaspoon salt, and plenty of pepper. Stir well.

c) If you are using fresh artichokes, prepare a bowl with water and the juice of ½ lemon. Remove the stalk from the artichoke and pull off the tough outer leaves. Once you reach the softer, pale leaves, use a large sharp knife to cut across the flower so that you are left with the bottom quarter. Use a small, sharp knife or a vegetable peeler to remove the outer layers of the artichoke until the base, or bottom, is exposed. Scrape out the hairy "choke" and put the base in the acidulated water. Discard the rest, then repeat with the other artichokes.

d) Put 2 tablespoons of the olive oil in a saucepan wide enough to hold the artichokes lying flat and heat over medium heat. Fill each artichoke bottom with 1 to 2 tablespoons of the beef mixture, pressing the filling in. Gently roll the bottoms in some flour, coating lightly and shaking off the excess. Fry in the hot oil for 1½ minutes on each side. Wipe the pan clean and return the artichokes to the pan, arranging them flat and snugly side by side.

e) Mix the stock, lemon juice, and the remaining oil and season generously with salt and pepper. Ladle spoonfuls of the liquid over the artichokes until they are almost, but not completely, submerged; you may not need all the liquid. Place a piece of parchment paper over the artichokes, cover the pan with a lid, and simmer over low heat for 1 hour. When they're ready, only about 4 tablespoons liquid should remain. If necessary, remove the lid and paper and reduce the sauce. Set the pan aside until the artichokes are just warm or at room temperature.

f) When ready to serve, blanch the peas for 2 minutes. Drain and add them and the dill to the pan with the artichokes, season to taste, and mix everything together gently.

75. Roasted Chicken with Jerusalem Artichoke

Makes: 4

INGREDIENTS
- 1 lb / 450 g Jerusalem artichokes, peeled and cut lengthwise into 6 wedges ⅔ inch / 1.5 cm thick
- 3 tbsp freshly squeezed lemon juice
- 8 skin-on, bone-in chicken thighs, or 1 medium whole chicken, quartered
- 12 banana or other large shallots, halved lengthwise
- 12 large cloves garlic, sliced
- 1 medium lemon, halved lengthwise and then very thinly sliced
- 1 tsp saffron threads
- 3½ tbsp / 50 ml olive oil
- ¾ cup / 150 ml cold water
- 1¼ tbsp pink peppercorns, lightly crushed
- ¼ cup / 10 g fresh thyme leaves
- 1 cup / 40 g tarragon leaves, chopped
- 2 tsp salt
- ½ tsp freshly ground black pepper

INSTRUCTIONS

a) Put the Jerusalem artichokes in a medium saucepan, cover with plenty of water, and add half the lemon juice. Bring to a boil, lower the heat, and simmer for 10 to 20 minutes, until tender but not soft. Drain and leave to cool.

b) Place the Jerusalem artichokes and all the remaining ingredients, excluding the remaining lemon juice and half of the tarragon, in a large mixing bowl and use your hands to mix everything together well. Cover and leave to marinate in the fridge overnight, or for at least 2 hours.

c) Preheat the oven to 475°F / 240°C. Arrange the chicken pieces, skin side up, in the center of a roasting pan and spread the remaining ingredients around the chicken. Roast for 30 minutes. Cover the pan with aluminum foil and cook for a further 15 minutes. At this point, the chicken should be completely cooked. Remove from the oven and add the reserved tarragon and lemon juice. Stir well, taste, and add more salt if needed. Serve at once.

76. Poached chicken with freekeh

Makes: 4 GENEROUSLY

INGREDIENTS
- 1 small free-range chicken, about 3¼ lb / 1.5 kg
- 2 long cinnamon sticks
- 2 medium carrots, peeled and cut into slices ¾ inch / 2 cm thick
- 2 bay leaves
- 2 bunches flat-leaf parsley (about 2½ oz / 70 g in total)
- 2 large onions
- 2 tbsp olive oil
- 2 cups / 300 g cracked freekeh
- ½ tsp ground allspice
- ½ tsp ground coriander
- 2½ tbsp / 40 g unsalted butter
- ⅔ cup / 60 g sliced almonds
- salt and freshly ground black pepper

INSTRUCTIONS

a) Place the chicken in a large pot, along with the cinnamon, carrots, bay leaves, 1 bunch of parsley, and 1 teaspoon salt. Quarter 1 onion and add it to the pot. Add cold water to almost cover the chicken; bring to a boil and simmer, covered, for 1 hour, occasionally skimming any oil and froth away from the surface.

b) About halfway through the cooking of the chicken, slice the second onion thinly and place it in a medium saucepan with the olive oil. Fry over medium-low heat for 12 to 15 minutes, until the onion turns golden brown and soft. Add the freekeh, allspice, coriander, ½ teaspoon salt, and some black pepper. Stir well and then add 2½ cups / 600 ml of the chicken broth. Turn the heat up to medium-high. As soon as the broth boils, cover the pan and lower the heat. Simmer gently for 20 minutes, then remove from the heat and leave covered for 20 minutes more.

c) Remove the leaves from the remaining parsley bunch and chop them up, not too fine. Add most of the chopped parsley to the cooked freekeh, mixing it in with a fork.
d) Lift the chicken out of the broth and place it on a cutting board. Carefully carve off the breasts and slice them thinly at an angle; remove the meat from the legs and thighs. Keep the chicken and the freekeh warm.
e) When ready to serve, place the butter, almonds, and some salt in a small frying pan and fry until golden. Spoon the freekeh onto individual serving dishes or one platter. Top with the leg and thigh meat, then arrange the breast slices neatly on top. Finish with the almonds and butter and a sprinkle of parsley.

77. Chicken with Onion & Cardamom Rice

Makes: 4

INGREDIENTS
- 3 tbsp / 40 g sugar
- 3 tbsp / 40 ml water
- 2½ tbsp / 25 g barberries (or currants)
- 4 tbsp olive oil
- 2 medium onions, thinly sliced (2 cups / 250 g in total)
- 2¼ lb / 1 kg skin-on, bone-in chicken thighs, or 1 whole chicken, quartered
- 10 cardamom pods
- rounded ¼ tsp whole cloves
- 2 long cinnamon sticks, broken in two
- 1⅔ cups / 300 g basmati rice
- 2¼ cups / 550 ml boiling water
- 1½ tbsp / 5 g flat-leaf parsley leaves, chopped
- ½ cup / 5 g dill leaves, chopped
- ¼ cup / 5 g cilantro leaves, chopped
- ⅓ cup / 100 g Greek yogurt, mixed with 2 tbsp olive oil (optional)
- salt and freshly ground black pepper

INSTRUCTIONS

a) Put the sugar and water in a small saucepan and heat until the sugar dissolves. Remove from the heat, add the barberries, and set aside to soak. If using currants, you do not need to soak them in this way.

b) Meanwhile, heat half the olive oil in a large sauté pan for which you have a lid over medium heat, add the onion, and cook for 10 to 15 minutes, stirring occasionally, until the onion has turned a deep golden brown. Transfer the onion to a small bowl and wipe the pan clean.

c) Place the chicken in a large mixing bowl and season with 1½ teaspoons each salt and black pepper. Add the remaining olive oil, cardamom, cloves, and cinnamon and use your hands to mix everything together well. Heat the frying pan again and place the chicken and spices in it. Sear for 5 minutes on each side and remove from the pan (this is important as it part-cooks the chicken). The spices can stay in the pan, but don't worry if they stick to the chicken. Remove most of the remaining oil as well, leaving just a thin film at the bottom. Add the rice, caramelized onion, 1 teaspoon salt, and plenty of black pepper. Drain the barberries and add them as well. Stir well and return the seared chicken to the pan, pushing it into the rice.

d) Pour the boiling water over the rice and chicken, cover the pan, and cook over very low heat for 30 minutes. Take the pan off the heat, remove the lid, quickly place a clean tea towel over the pan, and seal again with the lid. Leave the dish undisturbed for another 10 minutes. Finally, add the herbs and use a fork to stir them in and fluff up the rice. Taste and add more salt and pepper if needed. Serve hot or warm with yogurt if you like.

78. Chopped liver

Makes: 4 TO 6

INGREDIENTS
- 6½ tbsp / 100 ml melted goose or duck fat
- 2 large onions, sliced (about 3 cups / 400 g in total)
- 14 oz / 400 g chicken livers, cleaned and broken down into roughly 1¼-inch / 3cm chunks
- 5 extra-large free-range eggs, hard boiled
- 4 tbsp dessert wine
- 1 tsp salt
- ½ tsp freshly ground black pepper
- 2 to 3 green onions, thinly sliced
- 1 tbsp chopped chives

INSTRUCTIONS

a) Place two-thirds of the goose fat in a large frying pan and fry the onions over medium heat for 10 to 15 minutes, stirring occasionally, until dark brown. Remove the onions from the pan, pushing them down a little as you do so, so that you are left with some fat in the pan. Add a little fat if needed. Add the livers and cook them for up to 10 minutes, stirring from time to time, until they are properly cooked in the middle—no blood should be coming out at this stage.

b) Mix the livers with the onion before chopping them together. The best way to do this is with a meat grinder, processing the mixture twice to get the right texture. If you don't have a meat grinder, a food processor is also fine. Blitz the onions and liver in two or three batches so the machine bowl isn't very full. Pulse for 20 to 30 seconds, then check, making sure the liver and onions have turned into a uniformly smooth, yet still "bumpy" paste. Transfer everything into a large mixing bowl.

c) Peel the eggs, then grate two of them roughly and another two finely and add them to the liver mixture. Add the remaining fat, the dessert wine, and the salt and pepper and fold everything together gently. Transfer the mix to a nonmetallic flat dish and cover the surface tightly with plastic wrap. Leave it to cool down, then store in the fridge for at least 2 hours to firm up a little.

d) To serve, finely chop the remaining egg. Spoon the chopped liver onto individual serving plates, garnish with the chopped egg, and sprinkle with the green onions and chives.

79. Saffron Chicken & Herb Salad

Makes: 6

INGREDIENTS
- 1 orange
- 2½ tbsp / 50 g honey
- ½ tsp saffron threads
- 1 tbsp white wine vinegar
- 1¼ cups / about 300 ml water
- 2¼ lb / 1 kg skinless, boneless chicken breast
- 4 tbsp olive oil
- 2 small fennel bulbs, thinly sliced
- 1 cup / 15 g picked cilantro leaves
- ⅔ cup / 15 g picked basil leaves, torn
- 15 picked mint leaves, torn
- 2 tbsp freshly squeezed lemon juice
- 1 red chile, thinly sliced
- 1 clove garlic, crushed
- salt and freshly ground black pepper

INSTRUCTIONS

a) Preheat the oven to 400°F / 200°C. Trim and discard ⅜ inch / 1 cm off the top and tail of the orange and cut it into 12 wedges, keeping the skin on. Remove any seeds.

b) Place the wedges in a small saucepan with the honey, saffron, vinegar, and just enough water to cover the orange wedges. Bring to a boil and simmer gently for about an hour. At the end you should be left with soft orange and about 3 tablespoons of thick syrup; add water during the cooking if the liquid gets very low. Use a food processor to blitz the orange and syrup into a smooth, runny paste; again, add a little water if needed.

c) Mix the chicken breast with half the olive oil and plenty of salt and pepper and place on a very hot ridged griddle pan. Sear for about 2 minutes on each side to get clear char marks all over. Transfer to a roasting pan and place in the oven for 15 to 20 minutes, until just cooked.

d) Once the chicken is cool enough to handle but still warm, tear it with your hands into rough, quite large pieces. Place in a large mixing bowl, pour over half the orange paste, and stir well. (The other half you can keep in the fridge for a few days. It would make a good addition to an herb salsa to serve with oily fish such as mackerel or salmon.) Add the remaining ingredients to the salad, including the rest of the olive oil, and toss gently. Taste, add salt and pepper, and, if needed, more olive oil and lemon juice.

80. Hannukah Chicken sofrito

INGREDIENTS
- 1 tbsp sunflower oil
- 1 small free-range chicken, about 3¼ lb / 1.5 kg, butterflied or quartered
- 1 tsp sweet paprika
- ¼ tsp ground turmeric
- ¼ tsp sugar
- 2½ tbsp freshly squeezed lemon juice
- 1 large onion, peeled and quartered
- sunflower oil, for frying
- 1⅔ lb / 750 g Yukon Gold potatoes, peeled, washed, and cut into ¾-inch / 2cm dice
- 25 cloves garlic, unpeeled
- salt and freshly ground black pepper

INSTRUCTIONS

a) Pour the oil into a large, shallow pan or Dutch oven and put over medium heat. Place the chicken flat in the pan, skin side down, and sear for 4 to 5 minutes, until golden brown. Season all over with the paprika, turmeric, sugar, ¼ teaspoon salt, a good grind of black pepper, and 1½ tablespoons of the lemon juice. Turn the chicken over so that the skin faces up, add the onion to the pan, and cover with a lid. Decrease the heat to low and cook for a total of about 1½ hours; this includes the time the chicken is cooked with the potatoes. Lift the lid every now and then to check the amount of liquid in the bottom of the pan. The idea is for the chicken to cook and steam in its own juices, but you may need to add a little bit of boiling water, just so that there is always ¼ inch / 5 mm of liquid at the bottom of the pan.

b) After the chicken has been cooking for about 30 minutes, pour sunflower oil into a medium saucepan to a depth of 1¼ inches / 3 cm and place over medium-high heat. Fry the potatoes and garlic together in a few batches for about 6 minutes per batch, until they take on some color and crisp up. Use a slotted spoon to lift each batch away from the oil and onto paper towels, then sprinkle with salt.

c) After the chicken has been cooking for 1 hour, lift it from the pan and spoon in the fried potatoes and garlic, stirring them with the cooking juices. Return the chicken to the pan, placing it on top of the potatoes for the remainder of the cooking time, that is, 30 minutes. The chicken should be falling off the bone and the potatoes should be soaked in the cooking liquid and completely soft. Drizzle with the remaining lemon juice when serving.

81. <u>Hannukah</u> Kofta B'siniyah

Makes: 18 KOFTA

INGREDIENTS
- ⅔ cup / 150 g light tahini paste
- 3 tbsp freshly squeezed lemon juice
- ½ cup / 120 ml water
- 1 medium clove garlic, crushed
- 2 tbsp sunflower oil
- 2 tbsp / 30 g unsalted butter or ghee (optional)
- toasted pine nuts, to garnish
- finely chopped flat-leaf parsley, to garnish
- sweet paprika, to garnish
- salt

KOFTA
- 14 oz / 400 g ground lamb
- 14 oz / 400 g ground veal or beef
- 1 small onion (about 5 oz / 150 g), finely chopped
- 2 large cloves garlic, crushed
- 7 tbsp / 50 g toasted pine nuts, coarsely chopped
- ½ cup / 30 g finely chopped flat-leaf parsley
- 1 large medium-hot red chile, seeded and finely chopped
- 1½ tsp ground cinnamon
- 1½ tsp ground allspice
- ¾ tsp grated nutmeg
- 1½ tsp freshly ground black pepper
- 1½ tsp salt

INSTRUCTIONS

a) Put all the kofta ingredients in a bowl and use your hands to mix everything together well. Now shape into long, torpedo-like fingers, roughly 3¼ inches / 8 cm long (about 2 oz / 60 g each). Press the mix to compress it and ensure each kofta is tight and keeps its shape. Arrange on a plate and chill until you are ready to cook them, for up to 1 day.

b) Preheat the oven to 425°F / 220°C. In a medium bowl, whisk together the tahini paste, lemon juice, water, garlic, and ¼ teaspoon salt. The sauce should be a bit runnier than honey; add 1 to 2 tablespoons water if needed.
c) Heat the sunflower oil in a large frying pan over high heat and sear the kofta. Do this in batches so they are not cramped together. Sear them on all sides until golden brown, about 6 minutes per batch. At this point, they should be medium-rare. Lift out of the pan and arrange on a baking sheet. If you want to cook them medium or well done, put the baking sheet in the oven now for 2 to 4 minutes.
d) Spoon the tahini sauce around the kofta so it covers the base of the pan. If you like, also drizzle some over the kofta, but leave some of the meat exposed. Place in the oven for a minute or two, just to warm up the sauce a little.
e) Meanwhile, if you are using the butter, melt it in a small saucepan and allow it to brown a little, taking care that it doesn't burn. Spoon the butter over the kofta as soon as they come out of the oven. Scatter with the pine nuts and parsley and then sprinkle with the paprika. Serve at once.

82. Beef Meatballs with Fava Beans & Lemon

Makes: ABOUT 20 MEATBALLS

INGREDIENTS
- 4½ tbsp olive oil
- 2⅓ cups / 350 g fava beans, fresh or frozen
- 4 whole thyme sprigs
- 6 cloves garlic, sliced
- 8 green onions, cut at an angle into ¾-inch / 2cm segments
- 2½ tbsp freshly squeezed lemon juice
- 2 cups / 500 ml chicken stock
- salt and freshly ground black pepper
- 1½ tsp each chopped flat-leaf parsley, mint, dill, and cilantro, to finish

MEATBALLS
- 10 oz / 300 g ground beef
- 5 oz / 150 g ground lamb
- 1 medium onion, finely chopped
- 1 cup / 120 g bread crumbs
- 2 tbsp each chopped flat-leaf parsley, mint, dill, and cilantro
- 2 large cloves garlic, crushed
- 4 tsp baharat spice mix (store-bought or see recipe)
- 4 tsp ground cumin
- 2 tsp capers, chopped
- 1 egg, beaten

INSTRUCTIONS

a) Place all of the meatball ingredients in a large mixing bowl. Add ¾ teaspoon salt and plenty of black pepper and mix well with your hands. Form into balls about the same size as Ping-Pong balls. Heat 1 tablespoon of the olive oil over medium heat in an extra-large frying pan for which you have a lid. Sear half the meatballs, turning them until they are brown all over, about 5 minutes. Remove, add another 1½ teaspoons of the olive oil to the pan, and cook the other batch of meatballs. Remove from the pan and wipe it clean.

b) While the meatballs are cooking, throw the fava beans into a pot with plenty of salted boiling water and blanch for 2 minutes. Drain and refresh under cold water. Remove the skins from half the fava beans and discard the skins.
c) Heat the remaining 3 tablespoons olive oil over medium heat in the same pan in which you seared the meatballs. Add the thyme, garlic, and green onion and sauté for 3 minutes. Add the unpeeled fava beans, 1½ tablespoons of the lemon juice, ⅓ cup / 80 ml of the stock, ¼ teaspoon salt, and plenty of black pepper. The beans should be almost covered with liquid. Cover the pan and cook over low heat for 10 minutes.
d) Return the meatballs to the frying pan holding the fava beans. Add the remaining stock, cover the pan, and simmer gently for 25 minutes. Taste the sauce and adjust the seasoning. If it is very runny, remove the lid and reduce a little. Once the meatballs stop cooking, they will soak up a lot of the juices, so make sure there is still plenty of sauce at this point. You can leave the meatballs now, off the heat, until ready to serve.
e) Just before serving, reheat the meatballs and add a little water, if needed, to get enough sauce. Add the remaining herbs, the remaining 1 tablespoon lemon juice, and the peeled fava beans and stir very gently. Serve immediately.

83. Lamb Meatballs with Barberries, Yogurt & Herbs

Makes: ABOUT 20 MEATBALLS

INGREDIENTS
- 1⅔ lb / 750 g ground lamb
- 2 medium onions, finely chopped
- ⅔ oz / 20 g flat-leaf parsley, finely chopped
- 3 cloves garlic, crushed
- ¾ tsp ground allspice
- ¾ tsp ground cinnamon
- 6 tbsp / 60 g barberries
- 1 large free-range egg
- 6½ tbsp / 100 ml sunflower oil
- 1½ lb / 700 g banana or other large shallots, peeled
- ¾ cup plus 2 tbsp / 200 ml white wine
- 2 cups / 500 ml chicken stock
- 2 bay leaves
- 2 thyme sprigs
- 2 tsp sugar
- 5 oz / 150 g dried figs
- 1 cup / 200 g Greek yogurt
- 3 tbsp mixed mint, cilantro, dill, and tarragon, coarsely torn
- salt and freshly ground black pepper

INSTRUCTIONS
a) Place the lamb, onions, parsley, garlic, allspice, cinnamon, barberries, egg, 1 teaspoon salt, and ½ teaspoon black pepper in a large bowl. Mix with your hands, then roll into balls about the size of golf balls.

b) Heat one-third of the oil over medium heat in a large, heavy-bottomed pot for which you have a tight-fitting lid. Put in a few meatballs and cook and turn them around for a few minutes until they color all over. Remove from the pot and set aside. Cook the remaining meatballs the same way.

c) Wipe the pot clean and add the remaining oil. Add the shallots and cook them over medium heat for 10 minutes, stirring frequently, until golden brown. Add the wine, leave to bubble for a minute or two, then add the chicken stock, bay leaves, thyme, sugar, and some salt and pepper. Arrange the figs and meatballs among and on top of the shallots; the meatballs need to be almost covered in liquid. Bring to a boil, cover with the lid, decrease the heat to very low, and leave to simmer for 30 minutes. Remove the lid and simmer for about another hour, until the sauce has reduced and intensified in flavor. Taste and add salt and pepper if needed.

d) Transfer to a large, deep serving dish. Whisk the yogurt, pour on top, and scatter with the herbs.

84. Turkey & Zucchini Burgers with Green Onion & Cumin

Makes: ABOUT 18 BURGERS

INGREDIENTS
- 1 lb / 500 g ground turkey
- 1 large zucchini, coarsely grated (2 cups / 200 g in total)
- 3 green onions, thinly sliced
- 1 large free-range egg
- 2 tbsp chopped mint
- 2 tbsp chopped cilantro
- 2 cloves garlic, crushed
- 1 tsp ground cumin
- 1 tsp salt
- ½ tsp freshly ground black pepper
- ½ tsp cayenne pepper
- about 6½ tbsp / 100 ml of sunflower oil, for searing

SOUR CREAM & SUMAC SAUCE
- ½ cup / 100 g sour cream
- ⅔ cup / 150 g Greek yogurt
- 1 tsp grated lemon zest
- 1 tbsp freshly squeezed lemon juice
- 1 small clove garlic, crushed
- 1½ tbsp olive oil
- 1 tbsp sumac
- ½ tsp salt
- ¼ tsp freshly ground black pepper

INSTRUCTIONS

a) First make the sour cream sauce by placing all the ingredients in a small bowl. Stir well and set aside or chill until needed.

b) Preheat the oven to 425°F / 220°C. In a large bowl, combine all the ingredients for the meatballs except the sunflower oil. Mix with your hands and then shape into about 18 burgers, each weighing about 1½ oz / 45 g.

c) Pour enough sunflower oil into a large frying pan to form a layer about 1/16 inch / 2 mm thick on the pan bottom. Heat over medium heat until hot, then sear the meatballs in batches on all sides. Cook each batch for about 4 minutes, adding oil as needed, until golden brown.

d) Carefully transfer the seared meatballs to a baking sheet lined with waxed paper and place in the oven for 5 to 7 minutes, or until just cooked through. Serve warm or at room temperature, with the sauce spooned over or on the side.

85. Polpettone

Makes: 8

INGREDIENTS
- 3 large free-range eggs
- 1 tbsp chopped flat-leaf parsley
- 2 tsp olive oil
- 1 lb / 500 g ground beef
- 1 cup / 100 g bread crumbs
- ½ cup / 60 g unsalted pistachios
- ½ cup / 80 g gherkins (3 or 4), cut into ⅜-inch / 1cm pieces
- 7 oz / 200 g cooked beef tongue (or ham), thinly sliced
- 1 large carrot, cut into chunks
- 2 celery stalks, cut into chunks
- 1 thyme sprig
- 2 bay leaves
- ½ onion, sliced
- 1 tsp chicken stock base
- boiling water, to cook
- salt and freshly ground black pepper

SALSINA VERDE
- 2 oz / 50 g flat-leaf parsley sprigs
- 1 clove garlic, crushed
- 1 tbsp capers
- 1 tbsp freshly squeezed lemon juice
- 1 tbsp white wine vinegar
- 1 large free-range egg, hard boiled and peeled
- ⅔ cup / 150 ml olive oil
- 3 tbsp bread crumbs, preferably fresh
- salt and freshly ground black pepper

INSTRUCTIONS

a) Start by making a flat omelet. Whisk together 2 of the eggs, the chopped parsley, and a pinch of salt. Heat the olive oil in a large frying pan (about 11 inches / 28 cm in diameter) over medium heat and pour in the eggs. Cook for 2 to 3 minutes, without stirring, until the eggs set into a thin omelet. Set aside to cool down.

b) In a large bowl, mix together the beef, bread crumbs, pistachios, gherkins, the remaining egg, 1 teaspoon salt, and ½ teaspoon pepper. Lay a large clean tea towel (you may want to use an old one you don't mind getting rid of; cleaning it will be a slight menace) over your work surface. Now take the meat mix and spread it on the towel, shaping it with your hands into a rectangular disk, ⅜ inch / 1 cm thick and roughly 12 by 10 inches / 30 by 25 cm. Keep the edges of the cloth clear.

c) Cover the meat with the tongue slices, leaving ¾ inch / 2 cm around the edge. Cut the omelet into 4 wide strips and spread them evenly over the tongue.

d) Lift the cloth to help you start rolling the meat inward from one of its wide sides. Continue rolling the meat into a large sausage shape, using the towel to assist you. In the end you want a tight, jelly-roll-like loaf, with the ground beef on the outside and the omelet in the center. Cover the loaf with the towel, wrapping it up well so it is sealed inside. Tie the ends with string and tuck any excess cloth underneath the log so you end up with a tightly bound bundle.

e) Place the bundle inside a large pan or Dutch oven. Throw the carrot, celery, thyme, bay, onion, and stock base around the loaf and pour over boiling water to almost cover it. Cover the pot with a lid and leave to simmer for 2 hours.

f) Remove the loaf from the pan and set it aside to allow some of the liquid to drain (the poaching stock would make a great soup base). After about 30 minutes, place something heavy on top to remove more of the juices. Once it reaches room temperature, put the meat loaf in the fridge, still covered in cloth, to chill thoroughly, 3 to 4 hours.

g) For the sauce, put all the ingredients in a food processor and pulse to a coarse consistency (or, for a rustic look, chop the parsley, capers, and egg by hand and stir together with the rest of the ingredients). Taste and adjust the seasoning.

h) To serve, remove the loaf from the towel, cut into slices ⅜ inch / 1 cm thick, and layer on a serving plate. Serve the sauce on the side.

86. Braised Eggs with Lamb, Tahini & Sumac

Makes: 4

INGREDIENTS
- 1 tbsp olive oil
- 1 large onion, finely chopped (1¼ cups / 200 g in total)
- 6 cloves garlic, sliced thinly
- 10 oz / 300 g ground lamb
- 2 tsp sumac, plus extra to finish
- 1 tsp ground cumin
- ½ cup / 50 g toasted unsalted pistachios, crushed
- 7 tbsp / 50 g toasted pine nuts
- 2 tsp harissa paste (store-bought or see recipe)
- 1 tbsp finely chopped preserved lemon peel (store-bought or see recipe)
- 1⅓ cups / 200 g cherry tomatoes
- ½ cup / 120 ml chicken stock
- 4 large free-range eggs
- ¼ cup / 5 g picked cilantro leaves, or 1 tbsp Zhoug
- salt and freshly ground black pepper

YOGURT SAUCE
- ½ cup / 100 g Greek yogurt
- 1½ tbsp / 25 g tahini paste
- 2 tbsp freshly squeezed lemon juice
- 1 tbsp water

INSTRUCTIONS
a) Heat the olive oil over medium-high heat in a medium, heavy-bottomed frying pan for which you have a tight-fitting lid. Add the onion and garlic and sauté for 6 minutes to soften and color a bit. Raise the heat to high, add the lamb, and brown well, 5 to 6 minutes. Season with the sumac, cumin, ¾ teaspoon salt, and some black pepper and cook for another minute. Turn off the heat, stir in the nuts, harissa, and preserved lemon and set aside.

b) While the onion is cooking, heat a separate small cast-iron or other heavy pan over high heat. Once piping hot, add the cherry tomatoes and char for 4 to 6 minutes, tossing them in the pan occasionally, until slightly blackened on the outside. Set aside.

c) Prepare the yogurt sauce by whisking together all the ingredients with a pinch of salt. It needs to be thick and rich, but you may need to add a splash of water if it is stiff.

d) You can leave the meat, tomatoes, and sauce at this stage for up to an hour. When you are ready to serve, reheat the meat, add the chicken stock, and bring to a boil. Make 4 small wells in the mix and break an egg into each well. Cover the pan and cook the eggs over low heat for 3 minutes. Place the tomatoes on top, avoiding the yolks, cover again, and cook for 5 minutes, until the egg whites are cooked but the yolks are still runny.

e) Remove from the heat and dot with dollops of the yogurt sauce, sprinkle with sumac, and finish with the cilantro. Serve at once.

87. Slow-Cooked Veal with Prunes & Leek

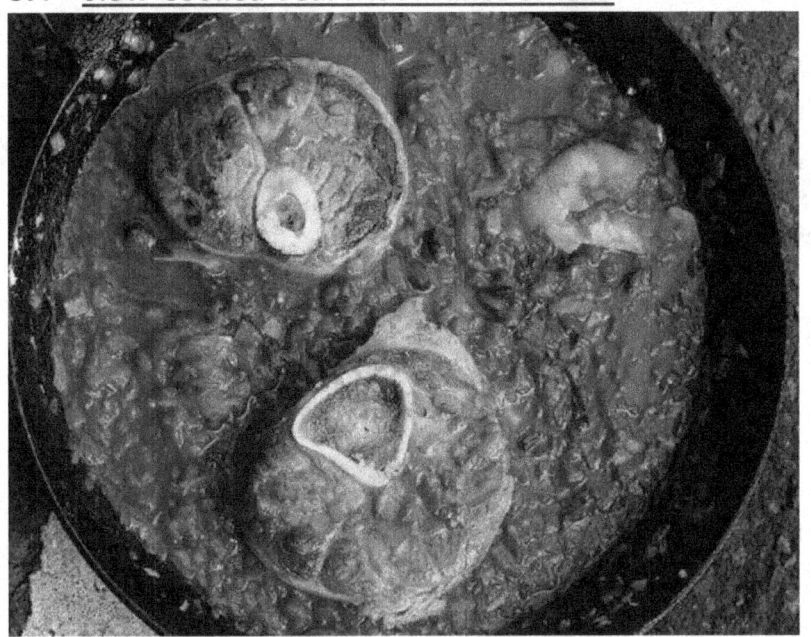

Makes: 4 GENEROUSLY

INGREDIENTS
- ½ cup / 110 ml sunflower oil
- 4 large osso buco steaks, on the bone (about 2¼ lb / 1 kg in total)
- 2 large onions, finely chopped (about 3 cups / 500 g in total)
- 3 cloves garlic, crushed
- 6½ tbsp / 100 ml dry white wine
- 1 cup / 250 ml chicken or beef stock
- one 14-oz / 400g can chopped tomatoes
- 5 thyme sprigs, leaves finely chopped
- 2 bay leaves
- zest of ½ orange, in strips
- 2 small cinnamon sticks
- ½ tsp ground allspice
- 2 star anise
- 6 large leeks, white part only (1¾ lb / 800 g in total), cut into ⅔-inch / 1.5cm slices
- 7 oz / 200 g soft prunes, pitted
- salt and freshly ground black pepper
- TO SERVE
- ½ cup / 120 g Greek yogurt
- 2 tbsp finely chopped flat-leaf parsley
- 2 tbsp grated lemon zest
- 2 cloves garlic, crushed

INSTRUCTIONS
a) Preheat the oven to 350°F / 180°C.
b) Heat 2 tablespoons of the oil in a large, heavy-bottomed pan over high heat. Fry the veal pieces for 2 minutes on each side, browning the meat well. Transfer to a colander to drain while you prepare the tomato sauce.
c) Remove most of the fat from the pan, add 2 more tablespoons of the oil, and add the onions and garlic. Return to medium-high heat and sauté, stirring occasionally and scraping the bottom of

the pan with a wooden spoon, for about 10 minutes, until the onions are soft and golden. Add the wine, bring to a boil, and simmer vigorously for 3 minutes, until most of it has evaporated. Add half the stock, the tomatoes, thyme, bay, orange zest, cinnamon, allspice, star anise, 1 teaspoon salt, and some black pepper. Stir well and bring to a boil. Add the veal pieces to the sauce and stir to coat.

d) Transfer the veal and sauce to a deep baking pan about 13 by 9½ inches / 33 by 24 cm, and spread it around evenly. Cover with aluminum foil and place in the oven for 2½ hours. Check a couple of times during the cooking to make sure the sauce is not becoming too thick and burning around the sides; you'll probably need to add a little water to prevent this. The meat is ready when it comes away easily from the bone. Lift the veal from the sauce and place it in a large bowl. When it is cool enough to handle, pick all the meat from the bones and use a small knife to scrape out all the marrow. Discard the bones.

e) Heat the remaining oil in a separate frying pan and brown the leeks well over high heat for about 3 minutes, stirring occasionally. Spoon them over the tomato sauce. Next, in the pan in which you made the tomato sauce, mix together the prunes, the remaining stock, and the pulled meat and bone marrow and spoon this over the leeks. Re-cover with the foil and continue to cook for another hour. Once out of the oven, taste and season with salt and more black pepper if needed.

f) Serve hot, with cold yogurt spooned on top and sprinkled with a mixture of the parsley, lemon zest, and garlic.

88. Hannukah Lamb shawarma

Makes: 8

INGREDIENTS
- 2 tsp black peppercorns
- 5 whole cloves
- ½ tsp cardamom pods
- ¼ tsp fenugreek seeds
- 1 tsp fennel seeds
- 1 tbsp cumin seeds
- 1 star anise
- ½ cinnamon stick
- ½ whole nutmeg, grated
- ¼ tsp ground ginger
- 1 tbsp sweet paprika
- 1 tbsp sumac
- 2½ tsp Maldon sea salt
- 1 oz / 25 g fresh ginger, grated
- 3 cloves garlic, crushed
- ⅔ cup / 40 g chopped cilantro, stems and leaves
- ¼ cup / 60 ml freshly squeezed lemon juice
- ½ cup / 120 ml peanut oil
- 1 bone-in leg of lamb, about 5½ to 6½ lb / 2.5 to 3 kg
- 1 cup / 240 ml boiling water

INSTRUCTIONS

a) Put the first 8 ingredients in a cast-iron pan and dry-roast over medium-high heat for a minute or two, until the spices begin to pop and release their aromas. Take care not to burn them. Add the nutmeg, ginger, and paprika, toss for a few more seconds, just to heat them, then transfer to a spice grinder. Process the spices to a uniform powder. Transfer to a medium bowl and stir in all the remaining ingredients, except the lamb.

b) Use a small, sharp knife to score the leg of lamb in a few places, making slits ⅔ inch / 1.5 cm deep through the fat and meat to allow the marinade to seep in. Place in a large roasting pan and rub the marinade all over the lamb; use your hands to massage the meat well. Cover the pan with aluminum foil and leave aside for at least a couple of hours or, preferably, chill overnight.

c) Preheat the oven to 325°F / 170°C.

d) Put the lamb in the oven with its fatty side facing up and roast for a total of about 4½ hours, until the meat is completely tender. After 30 minutes of roasting, add the boiling water to the pan and use this liquid to baste the meat every hour or so. Add more water, as needed, making sure there is always about ¼ inch / 0.5 cm in the bottom of the pan. For the last 3 hours, cover the lamb with foil to prevent the spices from burning. Once done, remove the lamb from the oven and leave to rest for 10 minutes before carving and serving.

e) The best way to serve this, to our mind, is inspired by Israel's most renowned shakshuka eatery (SEE RECIPE), Dr Shakshuka, in Jaffa, owned by Bino Gabso. Take six individual pita pockets and brush them liberally inside with a spread made by mixing together ⅔ cup / 120 g chopped canned tomatoes, 2 teaspoons / 20 g harissa paste, 4 teaspoons / 20 g tomato paste, 1 tablespoon olive oil, and some salt and pepper. When the lamb is ready, warm the pitas in a hot ridged griddle pan until they get nice char marks on both sides. Slice the warm lamb and cut the slices into ⅔-inch / 1.5cm strips. Pile them high over each warm pita, spoon over some of the roasting liquids from the pan, reduced, and finish with chopped onion, chopped parsley, and a sprinkle of sumac. And don't forget the fresh cucumber and tomato. It's a heavenly dish.

89. Panfried Sea Bass with Harissa & Rose

Makes: 2 TO 4

INGREDIENTS
- 3 tbsp harissa paste (store-bought or see recipe)
- 1 tsp ground cumin
- 4 sea bass fillets, about 1 lb / 450 g in total, skinned and with pin bones removed
- all-purpose flour, for dusting
- 2 tbsp olive oil
- 2 medium onions, finely chopped
- 6½ tbsp / 100 ml red wine vinegar
- 1 tsp ground cinnamon
- 1 cup / 200 ml water
- 1½ tbsp honey
- 1 tbsp rose water
- ½ cup / 60 g currants (optional)
- 2 tbsp coarsely chopped cilantro (optional)
- 2 tsp small dried edible rose petals
- salt and freshly ground black pepper

INSTRUCTIONS

a) First marinate the fish. Mix together half the harissa paste, the ground cumin, and ½ teaspoon salt in a small bowl. Rub the paste all over the fish fillets and leave them to marinate for 2 hours in the fridge.

b) Dust the fillets with a little flour and shake off the excess. Heat the olive oil in a wide frying pan over medium-high heat and fry the fillets for 2 minutes on each side. You may need to do this in two batches. Set the fish aside, leave the oil in the pan, and add the onions. Stir as you cook for about 8 minutes, until the onions are golden.

c) Add the remaining harissa, the vinegar, the cinnamon, ½ teaspoon salt, and plenty of black pepper. Pour in the water, lower the heat, and let the sauce simmer gently for 10 to 15 minutes, until quite thick.

d) Add the honey and rose water to the pan along with the currants, if using, and simmer gently for a couple more minutes. Taste and adjust the seasoning and then return the fish fillets to the pan; you can slightly overlap them if they don't quite fit. Spoon the sauce over the fish and leave them to warm up in the simmering sauce for 3 minutes; you may need to add a few tablespoons of water if the sauce is very thick. Serve warm or at room temperature, sprinkled with the cilantro, if using, and the rose petals.

90. Fish & caper kebabs with burnt eggplant & lemon pickle

Makes: 12 KEBABS

INGREDIENTS
- 2 medium eggplants (about 1⅔ lb / 750 g in total)
- 2 tbsp Greek yogurt
- 1 clove garlic, crushed
- 2 tbsp chopped flat-leaf parsley
- about 2 tbsp sunflower oil, for frying
- 2 tsp Quick Pickled Lemons
- salt and freshly ground black pepper
- FISH KEBABS
- 14 oz / 400 g haddock or any other white fish fillets, skinned and pin bones removed
- ½ cup / 30 g fresh bread crumbs
- ½ large free-range egg, beaten
- 2½ tbsp / 20 g capers, chopped
- ⅔ oz / 20 g dill, chopped
- 2 green onions, finely chopped
- grated zest of 1 lemon
- 1 tbsp freshly squeezed lemon juice
- ¾ tsp ground cumin
- ½ tsp ground turmeric
- ½ tsp salt
- ¼ tsp ground white pepper

INSTRUCTIONS
a) Start with the eggplants. Burn, peel, and drain the eggplant flesh following the instructions in the Burnt eggplant with garlic, lemon, and pomegranate seeds recipe. Once well drained, coarsely chop the flesh and place in a mixing bowl. Add the yogurt, garlic, parsley, 1 teaspoon salt, and plenty of black pepper. Set aside.
b) Cut the fish into very thin slices, only about ⅙ inch / 2 mm thick. Cut the slices into tiny dice and put in a medium mixing bowl. Add the remaining ingredients and stir well. Dampen your hands

and shape the mixture into 12 patties or fingers, about 1½ oz / 45 g each. Arrange on a plate, cover with plastic wrap, and leave in the fridge for at least 30 minutes.

c) Pour enough oil into a frying pan to form a thin film on the bottom and place over medium-high heat. Cook the kebabs in batches for 4 to 6 minutes for each batch, turning until colored on all sides and cooked through.

d) Serve the kebabs while still hot, 3 per portion, alongside the burnt eggplant and a small amount of pickled lemon (careful, the lemons tend to dominate).

91. Panfried mackerel with golden beet & orange salsa

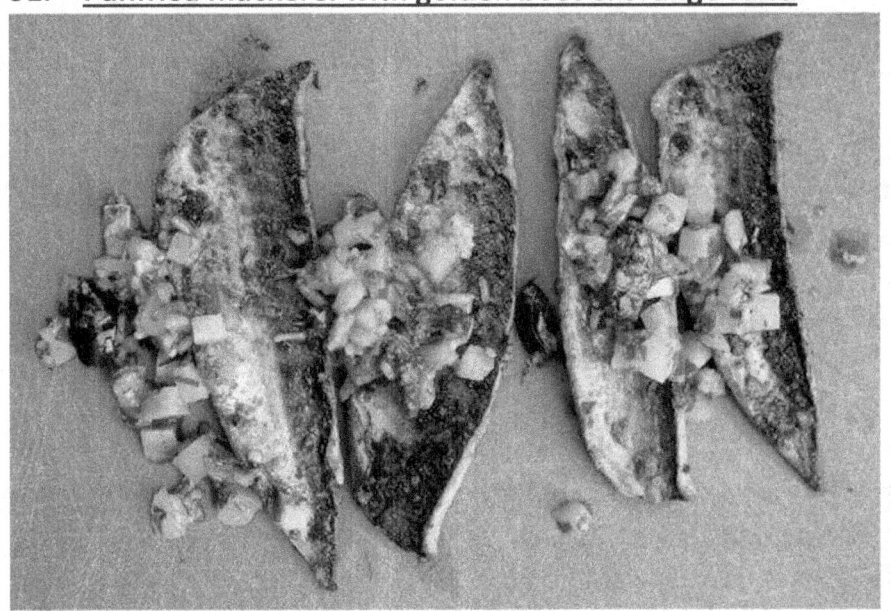

Makes: 4 AS A STARTER

INGREDIENTS
- 1 tbsp harissa paste (store-bought or see recipe)
- 1 tsp ground cumin
- 4 mackerel fillets (about 9 oz / 260 g in total), with skin
- 1 medium golden beet (3½ oz / 100 g in total)
- 1 medium orange
- 1 small lemon, halved widthwise
- ¼ cup / 30 g pitted Kalamata olives, quartered lengthwise
- ½ small red onion, finely chopped (¼ cup / 40 g in total)
- ¼ cup / 15 g chopped flat-leaf parsley
- ½ tsp coriander seeds, toasted and crushed
- ¾ tsp cumin seeds, toasted and crushed
- ½ tsp sweet paprika
- ½ tsp chile flakes
- 1 tbsp hazelnut or walnut oil
- ½ tsp olive oil
- salt

INSTRUCTIONS

a) Mix together the harissa paste, ground cumin, and a pinch of salt and rub the mixture into the mackerel fillets. Set aside in the fridge until ready to cook.

b) Boil the beet in plenty of water for about 20 minutes (it may take much longer, depending on the variety), until a skewer slides in smoothly. Allow to cool down, then peel, cut into ¼-inch / 0.5cm dice, and place in a mixing bowl.

c) Peel the orange and 1 lemon half, getting rid of all the outer pith, and cut them into quarters. Remove the middle pith and any seeds and cut the flesh into ¼-inch / 0.5cm dice. Add to the beet along with the olives, red onion, and parsley.

d) In a separate bowl, mix together the spices, the juice of the remaining lemon half, and the nut oil. Pour this onto the beet and orange mix, stir, and season to taste with salt. It's best to allow the salsa to stand at room temperature for at least 10 minutes to allow all the flavors to mingle.

e) Just before serving, heat the olive oil in a large nonstick frying pan over medium heat. Place the mackerel fillets skin side down in the pan, and cook, turning once, for about 3 minutes, until cooked through. Transfer to serving plates and spoon the salsa on top.

92. Cod Cakes in Tomato Sauce

Makes: 4

INGREDIENTS
- 3 slices white bread, crusts removed (about 2 oz / 60 g in total)
- 1⅓ lb / 600 g cod, halibut, hake, or pollock fillet, skinned and pin bones removed
- 1 medium onion, finely chopped (about 1 cup / 150 g in total)
- 4 cloves garlic, crushed
- 1 oz / 30 g flat-leaf parsley, finely chopped
- 1 oz / 30 g cilantro, finely chopped
- 1 tbsp ground cumin
- 1½ tsp salt
- 2 extra-large free-range eggs, beaten
- 4 tbsp olive oil
- TOMATO SAUCE
- 2½ tbsp olive oil
- 1½ tsp ground cumin
- ½ tsp sweet paprika
- 1 tsp ground coriander
- 1 medium onion, chopped
- ½ cup / 125 ml dry white wine
- one 14-oz / 400g can chopped tomatoes
- 1 red chile, seeded and finely chopped
- 1 clove garlic, crushed
- 2 tsp superfine sugar
- 2 tbsp mint leaves, coarsely chopped
- salt and freshly ground black pepper

INSTRUCTIONS

a) First, make the tomato sauce. Heat the olive oil over medium heat in a very large frying pan for which you have a lid. Add the spices and onion and cook for 8 to 10 minutes, until the onion is completely soft. Add the wine and simmer for 3 minutes. Add the tomatoes, chile, garlic, sugar, ½ teaspoon salt, and some black pepper. Simmer for about 15 minutes, until quite thick. Taste to adjust the seasoning and set aside.

b) While the sauce is cooking, make the fish cakes. Place the bread in a food processor and blitz to form bread crumbs. Chop the fish very finely and place in a bowl along with the bread and everything else, except the olive oil. Mix together well and then, using your hands, shape the mixture into compact cakes about ¾ inch / 2 cm thick and 3¼ inches / 8 cm in diameter. You should have 8 cakes. If they are very soft, refrigerate for 30 minutes to firm up. (You can also add some dried bread crumbs to the mix, though do this sparingly; the cakes need to be quite wet.)

c) Heat half the olive oil in a frying pan over medium-high heat, add half of the cakes, and sear for 3 minutes on each side, until well colored. Repeat with the remaining cakes and oil.

d) Gently place the seared cakes side by side in the tomato sauce; you can squeeze them a bit so they all fit. Add just enough water to cover the cakes partially (about a 1 cup / 200 ml). Cover the pan with the lid and simmer over very low heat for 15 to 20 minutes. Turn off the heat and leave the cakes to settle, uncovered, for at least 10 minutes before serving warm or at room temperature, sprinkled with the mint.

93. Grilled fish skewers with hawayej & parsley

Makes: 4 TO 6

INGREDIENTS
- 2¼ lb / 1 kg firm white fish fillets, such as monkfish or halibut, skinned, pin bones removed, and cut into 1-inch / 2.5cm cubes
- 1 cup / 50 g finely chopped flat-leaf parsley
- 2 large cloves garlic, crushed
- ½ tsp chile flakes
- 1 tbsp freshly squeezed lemon juice
- 2 tbsp olive oil
- salt
- lemon wedges, to serve
- 15 to 18 long bamboo skewers, soaked in water for 1 hour
- HAWAYEJ SPICE MIX
- 1 tsp black peppercorns
- 1 tsp coriander seeds
- 1½ tsp cumin seeds
- 4 whole cloves
- ½ tsp ground cardamom
- 1½ tsp ground turmeric

INSTRUCTIONS

a) Start with the hawayej mix. Place the peppercorns, coriander, cumin, and cloves in a spice grinder or mortar and work until finely ground. Add the ground cardamom and turmeric, stir well, and transfer to a large mixing bowl.

b) Place the fish, parsley, garlic, chile flakes, lemon juice, and 1 teaspoon salt in the bowl with the hawayej spices. Mix well with your hands, massaging the fish in the spice mixture until all pieces are well coated. Cover the bowl and, ideally, leave to marinate in the fridge for 6 to 12 hours. If you can't spare that time, don't worry; an hour should also be fine.

c) Place a ridged griddle pan over high heat and leave for about 4 minutes until hot. Meanwhile, thread the fish chunks onto the skewers, 5 to 6 pieces on each, making sure to leave gaps between the pieces. Gently brush the fish with a little olive oil and place the skewers on the hot griddle in 3 to 4 batches so they aren't too close together. Grill for about 1½ minutes on each side, until the fish is just cooked through. Alternatively, cook them on a grill or under a broiler, where they will take about 2 minutes on each side to cook.

d) Serve immediately with the lemon wedges.

94. Fricassee salad

Makes: 4

INGREDIENTS
- 4 rosemary sprigs
- 4 bay leaves
- 3 tbsp black peppercorns
- about 1⅔ cups / 400 ml extra virgin olive oil
- 10½ oz / 300 g tuna steak, in one piece or two
- 1⅓ lb / 600 g Yukon Gold potatoes, peeled and cut into ¾-inch / 2cm pieces
- ½ tsp ground turmeric
- 5 anchovy fillets, coarsely chopped
- 3 tbsp harissa paste (store-bought or see recipe)
- 4 tbsp capers
- 2 tsp finely chopped preserved lemon peel, (store-bought or see recipe)
- ½ cup / 60 g black olives, pitted and halved
- 2 tbsp freshly squeezed lemon juice
- 5 oz / 140 g preserved piquillo peppers (about 5 peppers), torn into rough strips
- 4 large eggs, hard boiled, peeled, and quartered
- 2 baby gem lettuces (about 5 oz / 140 g in total), leaves separated and torn
- ⅔ oz / 20 g flat-leaf parsley, leaves picked and torn
- salt

INSTRUCTIONS

a) To prepare the tuna, put the rosemary, bay leaves, and peppercorns in a small saucepan and add the olive oil. Heat the oil to just below the boiling point, when tiny bubbles begin to surface. Carefully add the tuna (the tuna must be completely covered; if it isn't, heat more oil and add to the pan). Remove from the heat and leave aside for a couple hours, uncovered, then cover the pan and refrigerate for at least 24 hours.

b) Cook the potatoes with the turmeric in plenty of salted boiling water for 10 to 12 minutes, until cooked. Drain carefully, making sure none of the turmeric water spills (the stains are a pain to remove!), and place in a large mixing bowl. While the potatoes are still hot, add the anchovies, harissa, capers, preserved lemon, olives, 6 tbsp / 90 ml of the tuna preserving oil, and some of the peppercorns from the oil. Mix gently and leave to cool.
c) Lift the tuna from the remaining oil, break it into bite-size chunks, and add to the salad. Add the lemon juice, peppers, eggs, lettuce, and parsley. Toss gently, taste, add salt if it needs it and possibly more oil, then serve.

95. Prawns, Scallops & Clams with Tomato & Feta

Makes: 4 AS A STARTER

INGREDIENTS
- 1 cup / 250 ml white wine
- 2¼ lb / 1 kg clams, scrubbed
- 3 cloves garlic, thinly sliced
- 3 tbsp olive oil, plus extra to finish
- 3½ cups / 600 g peeled and chopped Italian plum tomatoes (fresh or canned)
- 1 tsp superfine sugar
- 2 tbsp chopped oregano
- 1 lemon
- 7 oz / 200 g tiger prawns, peeled and deveined
- 7 oz / 200 g large scallops (if very large, cut in half horizontally)
- 4 oz / 120 g feta cheese, broken into ¾-inch / 2cm chunks
- 3 green onions, thinly sliced
- salt and freshly ground black pepper

INSTRUCTIONS

a) Place the wine in a medium saucepan and boil until reduced by three-quarters. Add the clams, cover immediately with a lid, and cook over high heat for about 2 minutes, shaking the pan occasionally, until the clams open. Transfer to a fine sieve to drain, capturing the cooking juices in a bowl. Discard any clams that don't open, then remove the remainder from their shells, leaving a few with their shells to finish the dish, if you like.

b) Preheat the oven to 475°F / 240°C.

c) In a large frying pan, cook the garlic in the olive oil over medium-high heat for about 1 minute, until golden. Carefully add the tomatoes, clam liquid, sugar, oregano, and some salt and pepper. Shave off 3 zest strips from the lemon, add them and simmer gently for 20 to 25 minutes, until the sauce thickens. Taste and add salt and pepper as needed. Discard the lemon zest.

d) Add the prawns and scallops, stir gently, and cook for just a minute or two. Fold in the shelled clams and transfer everything to a small ovenproof dish. Sink the feta pieces into the sauce and sprinkle with the green onion. Top with some clams in their shells, if you like, and place in the oven for 3 to 5 minutes, until the top colors a little and the prawns and scallops are just cooked. Remove the dish from the oven, squeeze a little lemon juice on top, and finish with a drizzle of olive oil.

96. Salmon Steaks in Chraimeh Sauce

Makes: 4

INGREDIENTS
- ½ cup / 110 ml sunflower oil
- 3 tbsp all-purpose flour
- 4 salmon steaks, about 1 lb / 950 g
- 6 cloves garlic, coarsely chopped
- 2 tsp sweet paprika
- 1 tbsp caraway seeds, dry toasted and freshly ground
- 1½ tsp ground cumin
- rounded ¼ tsp cayenne pepper
- rounded ¼ tsp ground cinnamon
- 1 green chile, coarsely chopped
- ⅔ cup / 150 ml water
- 3 tbsp tomato paste
- 2 tsp superfine sugar
- 1 lemon, cut into 4 wedges, plus 2 tbsp freshly squeezed lemon juice
- 2 tbsp coarsely chopped cilantro
- salt and freshly ground black pepper

INSTRUCTIONS

a) Heat 2 tablespoons of the sunflower oil over high heat in a large frying pan for which you have a lid. Place the flour in a shallow bowl, season generously with salt and pepper, and toss the fish in it. Shake off the excess flour and sear the fish for a minute or two on each side, until golden. Remove the fish and wipe the pan clean.

b) Place the garlic, spices, chile, and 2 tablespoons of the sunflower oil in a food processor and blitz to form a thick paste. You might need to add a little bit more oil to bring everything together.

c) Pour the remaining oil into the frying pan, heat well, and add the spice paste. Stir and fry for just 30 seconds, so that the spices don't burn. Quickly but carefully (it may spit!) add the water and tomato paste to stop the spices from cooking. Bring to a simmer and add the sugar, lemon juice, ¾ teaspoon salt, and some pepper. Taste for seasoning.

d) Put the fish in the sauce, bring to a gentle simmer, cover the pan and cook for 7 to 11 minutes, depending on the size of the fish, until it is just done. Remove the pan from the heat, take off the lid, and leave to cool down. Serve the fish just warm or at room temperature. Garnish each serving with the cilantro and a lemon wedge.

97. Marinated Sweet & Sour Fish

Makes: 4

INGREDIENTS
- 3 tbsp olive oil
- 2 medium onions, cut into ⅜-inch / 1cm slices (3 cups / 350 g in total)
- 1 tbsp coriander seeds
- 2 peppers (1 red and 1 yellow), halved lengthwise, seeded, and cut into strips ⅜ inch / 1 cm wide (3 cups / 300 g total)
- 2 cloves garlic, crushed
- 3 bay leaves
- 1½ tbsp curry powder
- 3 tomatoes, chopped (2 cups / 320 g in total)
- 2½ tbsp sugar
- 5 tbsp cider vinegar
- 1 lb / 500 g pollock, cod, halibut, haddock, or other white fish fillets, divided into 4 equal pieces
- seasoned all-purpose flour, for dusting
- 2 extra-large eggs, beaten
- ⅓ cup / 20 g chopped cilantro

salt and freshly ground black pepper

INSTRUCTIONS

a) Preheat the oven to 375°F / 190°C.
b) Heat 2 tablespoons of the olive oil in a large ovenproof frying pan or Dutch oven over medium heat. Add the onions and coriander seeds and cook for 5 minutes, stirring often. Add the peppers and cook for a further 10 minutes. Add the garlic, bay leaves, curry powder, and tomatoes, and cook for another 8 minutes, stirring occasionally. Add the sugar, vinegar, 1½ teaspoons salt, and some black pepper and continue to cook for another 5 minutes.
c) Meanwhile, heat the remaining 1 tablespoon oil in a separate frying pan over medium-high heat. Sprinkle the fish with some salt, dip in the flour, then in the eggs, and fry for about 3 minutes, turning once. Transfer the fish to paper towels to absorb the excess oil, then add to the pan with the peppers and onions, pushing the vegetables aside so the fish sits on the bottom of the pan. Add enough water just to immerse the fish (about 1 cup / 250 ml) in the liquid.
d) Place the pan in the oven for 10 to 12 minutes, until the fish is cooked. Remove from the oven and leave to cool to room temperature. The fish can now be served, but it is actually better after a day or two in the fridge. Before serving, taste and add salt and pepper, if needed, and garnish with the cilantro.

98. Red Pepper & Baked Egg Galettes

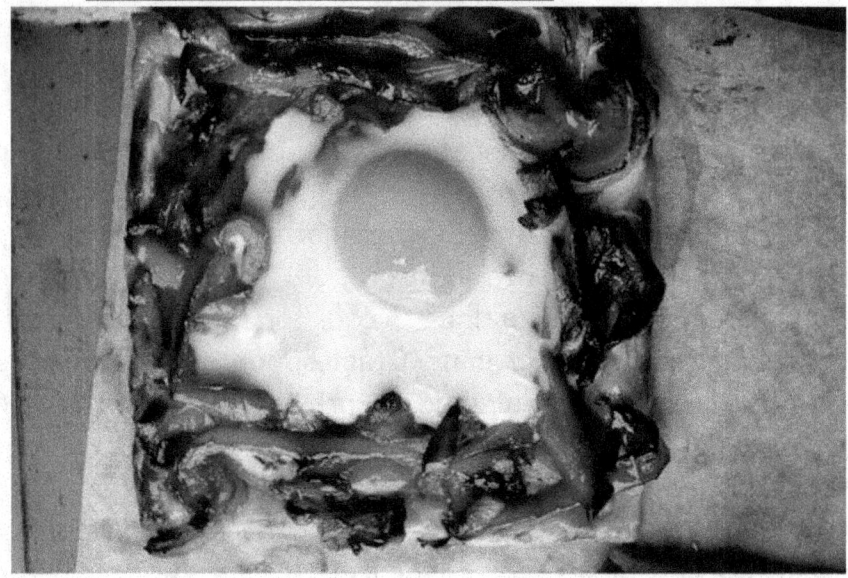

Makes: 4

INGREDIENTS
- 4 medium red peppers, halved, seeded, and cut into strips ⅜ inch / 1 cm wide
- 3 small onions, halved and cut into wedges ¾ inch / 2 cm wide
- 4 thyme sprigs, leaves picked and chopped
- 1½ tsp ground coriander
- 1½ tsp ground cumin
- 6 tbsp olive oil, plus extra to finish
- 1½ tbsp flat-leaf parsley leaves, coarsely chopped
- 1½ tbsp cilantro leaves, coarsely chopped
- 9 oz / 250 g best-quality, all-butter puff pastry
- 2 tbsp / 30 g sour cream
- 4 large free-range eggs (or 5½ oz / 160 g feta cheese, crumbled), plus 1 egg, lightly beaten
- salt and freshly ground black pepper

INSTRUCTIONS

a) Preheat the oven to 400°F / 210°C. In a large bowl, mix together the peppers, onions, thyme leaves, ground spices, olive oil, and a good pinch of salt. Spread out in a roasting pan and roast for 35 minutes, stirring a couple of times during the cooking. The vegetables should be soft and sweet but not too crisp or brown, as they will cook further. Remove from the oven and stir in half of the fresh herbs. Taste for seasoning and set aside. Turn the oven up to 425°F / 220°C.

b) On a lightly floured surface, roll out the puff pastry into a 12-inch / 30cm square about ⅛ inch / 3 mm thick and cut into four 6-inch / 15cm squares. Prick the squares all over with a fork and place them, well spaced, on a baking sheet lined with parchment paper. Leave to rest in the fridge for at least 30 minutes.

c) Remove the pastry from the fridge and brush the top and sides with beaten egg. Using an offset spatula or the back of a spoon, spread 1½ teaspoons of the sour cream over each square, leaving a ¼-inch / 0.5cm border around the edges. Arrange 3 tablespoons of the pepper mixture on top of the sour cream–topped squares, leaving the borders clear to rise. It should be spread fairly evenly, but leave a shallow well in the middle to hold an egg later on.

d) Bake the galettes for 14 minutes. Take the baking sheet out of the oven and carefully crack a whole egg into the well in the center of each pastry. Return to the oven and cook for another 7 minutes, until the eggs are just set. Sprinkle with black pepper and the remaining herbs and drizzle with oil. Serve at once.

99. <u>**Hannukah**</u> <u>Brick</u>

Makes: 2

INGREDIENTS
- about 1 cup / 250 ml sunflower oil
- 2 circles feuilles de brick pastry, 10 to 12 inches / 25 to 30 cm in diameter
- 3 tbsp chopped flat-leaf parsley
- 1½ tbsp chopped green onion, both green and white parts
- 2 large free-range eggs
- salt and freshly ground black pepper

INSTRUCTIONS
a) Pour the sunflower oil into a medium saucepan; it should come about ¾ inch / 2 cm up the sides of the pan. Place over medium heat and leave until the oil is hot. You don't want it too hot or the pastry will burn before the egg is cooked; tiny bubbles will start to surface when it reaches the right temperature.

b) Place one of the pastry circles inside a shallow bowl. (You can use a larger piece if you don't want to waste much pastry and fill it up more.) You will need to work quickly so that the pastry does not dry out and become stiff. Put half the parsley in the center of the circle and sprinkle with half the green onion. Create a little nest in which to rest an egg, then carefully crack an egg into the nest. Sprinkle generously with salt and pepper and fold in the sides of the pastry to create a parcel. The four folds will overlap so that the egg is fully enclosed. You can't seal the pastry, but a neat fold should keep the egg inside.

c) Carefully turn the parcel over and gently place it in the oil, seal side down. Cook for 60 to 90 seconds on each side, until the pastry is golden brown. The egg white should be set and the yolk still runny. Lift the cooked parcel from the oil and place between paper towels to soak up the excess oil. Keep warm while you cook the second pastry. Serve both parcels at once.

100. Sfiha or Lahm Bi'ajeen

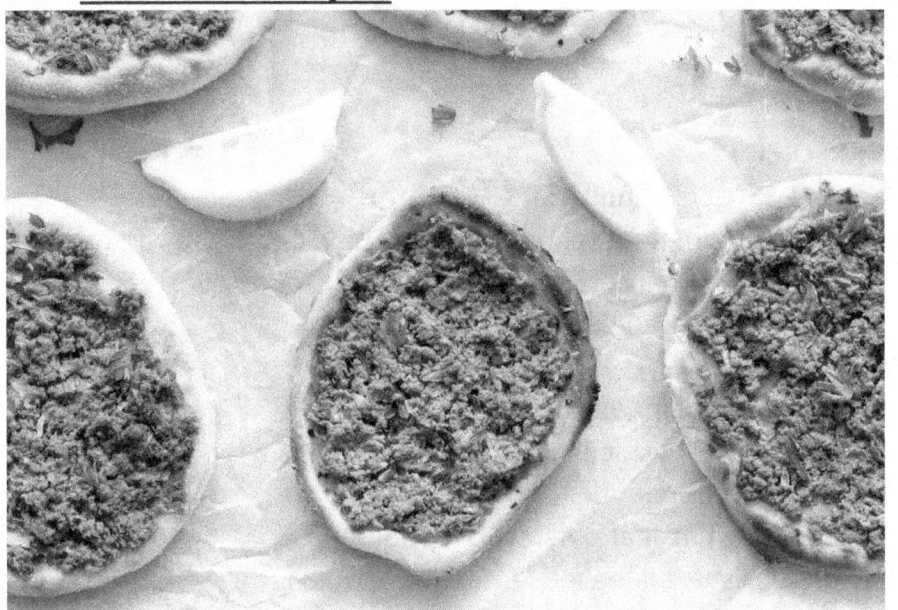

Makes: ABOUT 14 PASTRIES

TOPPING

INGREDIENTS
- 9 oz / 250 g ground lamb
- 1 large onion, finely chopped (1 heaping cup / 180 g in total)
- 2 medium tomatoes, finely chopped (1½ cups / 250 g)
- 3 tbsp light tahini paste
- 1¼ tsp salt
- 1 tsp ground cinnamon
- 1 tsp ground allspice
- ⅛ tsp cayenne pepper
- 1 oz / 25 g flat-leaf parsley, chopped
- 1 tbsp freshly squeezed lemon juice
- 1 tbsp pomegranate molasses
- 1 tbsp sumac
- 3 tbsp / 25 g pine nuts
- 2 lemons, cut into wedges

DOUGH
- 1⅔ cups / 230 g bread flour
- 1½ tbsp powdered milk
- ½ tbsp salt
- 1½ tsp fast-rising active dry yeast
- ½ tsp baking powder
- 1 tbsp sugar
- ½ cup / 125 ml sunflower oil
- 1 large free-range egg
- ½ cup / 110 ml lukewarm water
- olive oil, for brushing

INSTRUCTIONS

a) Start with the dough. Put the flour, powdered milk, salt, yeast, baking powder, and sugar in a large mixing bowl. Stir well to mix, then make a well in the center. Put the sunflower oil and egg in the well, then stir as you add the water. When the dough comes together, transfer it to a work surface and knead for 3 minutes, until elastic and uniform. Put in a bowl, brush with some olive oil, cover with a towel in a warm spot, and leave for 1 hour, at which point the dough should have risen a little.

b) In a separate bowl, use your hands to mix together all of the topping ingredients except the pine nuts and lemon wedges. Set aside.

c) Preheat the oven to 450°F / 230°C. Line a large baking sheet with parchment paper.

d) Divide the risen dough into 2-oz / 50g balls; you should have about 14. Roll out each ball into a circle about 5 inches / 12 cm in diameter and ⅙ inch / 2 mm thick. Brush each circle lightly on both sides with olive oil and place on the baking sheet. Cover and leave to rise for 15 minutes.

e) Use a spoon to divide the filling among the pastries, and spread it evenly so it covers the dough fully. Sprinkle with the pine nuts. Set aside to rise for another 15 minutes, then put in the oven for about 15 minutes, until just cooked. You want to make sure the pastry is just baked, not overbaked; the topping should be slightly pink inside and the pastry golden on the underside. Remove from the oven and serve warm or at room temperature with the lemon wedges.

CONCLUSION

Hanukkah recipes are an essential part of the celebration of this special holiday. They bring families and friends together to enjoy delicious, traditional dishes that have been passed down through generations. From crispy latkes to sweet sufganiyot, these recipes are full of flavor and symbolism. They represent the miracle of the oil, the warmth of family gatherings, and the joy of celebrating a holiday steeped in tradition. Whether you celebrate Hanukkah or simply want to try something new, these recipes are a wonderful way to experience the richness and depth of Jewish culture and cuisine.

www.ingramcontent.com/pod-product-compliance
Lightning Source LLC
Chambersburg PA
CBHW070650120526

44590CB00013BA/896